The Science
of
the Soul

The Science of the Soul

Consisting of

[Discourses and Excerpts from Letters]

SARDAR BAHADUR MAHARAJ JAGAT SINGH

RADHA SOAMI SATSANG BEAS

Published by:
Jagdish Chander Sethi, Secretary
Radha Soami Satsang Beas
Dera Baba Jaimal Singh
Punjab 143 204, India

Eleventh Edition 2002

09 08 07 06 05   8 7 6 5 4 3 2

ISBN 81-8256-022-5

Printed in India by: Lakshmi Offset Printers, Delhi-110092.

SARDAR BAHADUR MAHARAJ JAGAT SINGH JI

CONTENTS

PREFACE TO THE FOURTH EDITION

This wonderful book was first published in 1959 and in a space of a little over a decade has gone through three editions. The third edition was revised and considerably enlarged. The root of its popularity undoubtedly lies in the bold and forthright manner in which the author has set out the teachings of the Saints. In its range of appeal it covers a wide variety of persons—seekers and satsangis, alike—and all those who have spiritual aspirations. *A Spiritual Bouquet* section of the book has been further added to, for there has been an unceasing demand for this Ancient Wisdom which is the common heritage of the entire world. It is hoped that the fourth edition will go a long way towards fulfillment of the needs of those who are thirsting for spiritual knowledge.

K.L. Khanna

Radha Soami Satsang Beas
April 1972

PREFACE

Our two recent publications, that is, 'Spiritual Gems' and 'Light on Sant Mat' have been received with considerable enthusiasm and there has been a constant and overwhelming demand for literature, such as is to be found therein, both by Seekers and Satsangis as well as lovers of spiritual knowledge in India and abroad.

Encouraged by their appreciation, we are now presenting to the reader a collection, in book form, of well reasoned and illuminating discourses, and excerpts from letters and talks by Maharaj Jagat Singh Ji. He was, as the reader is no doubt now aware of, a Professor of Science, and His writings and talks have a scientific background.

Excerpts from Letters, it may be added, were selected by Maharaj Charan Singh Ji personally and the book is published under His scrutiny and care.

It is hoped that the book will be read with advantage by persons interested in spiritual advancement.

R. D. Ahluwalia,
Secretary.

Radha Soami Satsang Beas
October, 1959

FOREWORD

Maharaj Jagat Singh Ji, Sant Sat Guru, Radha Soami Satsang Beas (1948—1951) was born on the 27th July, 1884 at Nussi, a small village not very far from Beas. He received His education in the Mission School at Jullundur and later at the Government College, Lahore, where he took his M.Sc. degree in Chemistry. He joined the Punjab Agricultural College, Lyallpur, in 1911 as Assistant Professor of Chemistry and retired as Vice-Principal of the institution in 1943.

He was initiated in 1910 into the mystic practice of Surat Shabd Yoga or Nam Bhakti by Huzur Maharaj Baba Sawan Singh Ji. He practised it very assiduously and conscientiously and, even as a professor, He was popularly known among the staff as well as students as 'Guru Ji'. He had only two interests–His official duties and His spiritual practices, both of which were performed with unusual fervour. His faith in the Satguru was unshakable. Once, while in Lyallpur, he called on Sain Lasuri Shah, a highly evolved ascetic, with a message from Huzur Maharaj Baba Sawan Singh Ji. He used to carry such messages frequently between the two Mystics. The ascetic was so pleased with this particular message that he embraced Sardar Bahadur Ji and offered to open up the inner vision immediately. The offer, to which anybody would have succumbed, was politely but firmly declined with the words that His own Master would do this as and when He thought proper.

Unremitting in the discharge of His duties, He left the imprint of a masterly mind on whatever He undertook to do; and it would be no exaggeration to say that much of the reputation of the Lyallpur College was due to His painstaking efforts. His help and guidance was sought by all, irrespective of their position, and He was a tower of strength to the administration. Although extremely tender at heart, He was a strict disciplinarian whose sound judgment, humane methods and efficient handling of situations won Him high esteem and honour.

Always ready to pass on to others the credit due to Him, never standing for any show, He was unostentatious to an amazing degree. Many are the instances when He anonymously paid fees for students, even educated some abroad, without their having ever known who the donor was and without Himself knowing the donees.

Throughout His long service He had made it a point to spend most of the weekends with His Satguru (Baba Sawan Singh Ji Maharaj) at the Dera, and many a person in Lyallpur owes initiation from Huzur Maharaj Sawan Singh Ji to His solicitude for them.

After His retirement in 1943, He spent practically all His time in meditation and Shabd Abhyas (Practice) till He assumed charge of His Master's work at Beas in April 1948 and engrossed Himself fully in carrying out the functions and duties entrusted to Him, despite His indifferent health.

He talked little, used words sparingly, went straight to the point—often quite bluntly. At such moments, His quiet brown eyes would light up with a flash.

He attracted quite a large intelligentsia in India and abroad and, being both a scientist and a practical mystic, was able to satisfy their intellectual and spiritual hunger and make them abiding followers.

He passed away quietly early on the morning of the 23rd October, 1951. The day before, He had dictated His will and given instructions about His funeral. He wanted no show, no waiting for people to attend the cremation. The body was to be cremated within a few hours and the remains were to be consigned to the river on the same day. There is a custom in this country to bathe the dead body, anoint it with perfumes, etc., and cover it with a clean, new sheet of cloth. He completed this process very simply the night before His death by asking the doctor to give Him an enema, getting His body rubbed with a wet towel and changing into a clean suit. He had His bed moved from the centre of the room to a corner near the window, and ordered everybody out. There was a feeble knock on the window at about 3 a.m. He asked for a glass of water and then slept to wake up permanently into the higher worlds, to which He belonged.

His life was exemplary and one of absolute detachment from all material cravings. A true Karma Yogi in every sense of the word, He waded unruffled, almost with cynical indifference, through the muddy waters of the world, intent upon His own inner realization and on carrying out the Mission of His great Master.

Simple in His habits, frugal in His diet and faithful to His work, He invariably emphasized the practical and human side of life, and seldom missed a humorous situation. He would insist on 'vacating the body' as He termed it; that is, drawing the currents of consciousness up to the centre behind and above the eyes, and described it as the panacea for all ills of mind and body.

Such was Sardar Bahadur Maharaj Jagat Singh Ji, a collection of whose discourses, talks and excerpts from letters are now being placed before the reader of this book.

R. D. Ahluwalia

1959

PART I

Discourses

1

Who are Saints and what do they teach?

Today we shall discuss what is the true mission of Saints. In order to fully understand the subject, we must first have a clear conception of the term 'Saint' or 'Sant'. So many mistaken notions are current about Sant Mat that even a large number of educated people, including some leading exponents of various religious thoughts, do not seem to understand it clearly. The terms 'Sant', 'Saint' and 'Sadh' are so widely misunderstood that any beggar in saffron robes is loosely called a Sadh, which term was originally used to denote a person who is highly developed spiritually, and has crossed the regions of matter and mind.

It should be made clear at the outset that Sadhus do not recommend outward formalities, rites, rituals, modes of living, symbols or any special type of clothing. They are above castes, creeds, races, countries and nationalities. Nor is the term 'Saint' used in the sense in which it is generally applied in the Christian world; that is, one canonized by the Roman Catholic Church, or a holy person. As B.A. and M.A. are degrees connoting academic qualifications, so are the terms 'Saint' or 'Sant' and 'Sadh' degrees in the school of Spiritual Science. According to the teaching of the Saints :

1. *Bhekh* or Initiate is he who follows the Principles of Sant Mat and makes sincere efforts to tread the path of God-realization 'within', according to the instructions of the Master.

2. *Shishya* or *Sikh* is a disciple who has reached the first stage on the Way and who sees the Light of the Flame within. Guru Gobind Singh says: "A shishya is he who sees the Living Flame within himself."

3. *Gyani* is one who has reached the Brahm stage, which is the Fountainhead of all knowledge, whence the creation of the three gunas and the five tattwas begin. This is the highest stage of the yogis, gyanis and many religions of the world.

4. *Sadh* is one who has reached the Par Brahm Region. Kabir says, "Sadh is he who conquers this fort." The last census recorded the number of so-called sadhus in India at five million. But if you try to find the real Sadhs, perhaps you will not be to find even five. "None hath seen bags of diamonds, packs of lions, flocks of 'Hansas' or groups of Sadhs."

   —Kabir

5. *Sant* is He who has attained the highest stage and has become one with the Lord. The drop, having merged in the Ocean, has become the Ocean Itself. "God and God's men are one. There is no distinction."

   —Kabir

Paltu Sahib says :

Very near (and dear) to God are Saints.
Whatever they ordain, happens.
Yes, what they order, occurs;
For the Lord is within their command.
Whatever Saints ask, He does.

He never goes against Their wishes.
In the Mansion of the Lord,
All work is done by Saints.

Three hundred and thirty million gods,
Pay homage to Them.
They may turn a mole into a mountain,
Or reduce a mountain to a mole.

In the Lord's Mansion,
Their glory is ever proclaimed.
In fact, O Paltu ! in the Lord's House,
There is no other Doer.

Having defined the term 'Sant' or 'Saint', let us now consider what the teachings of the Saints are. Their first postulate, to whatever religion, race or clime they may belong, is: There is a God. The universe is not without a Creator, Sustainer and Protector. 'Sat Nam, Karta Purakh' (Guru Nanak). He is the Ocean of Bliss. He is eternal, birthless and deathless.

Secondly, all Saints teach that our soul is, in essence, a drop from the Ocean of the Lord, whence it separated so long ago as to have totally forgotten its Divine Origin. All its woe and misery will end only when it returns to its Original Home and merges in the Ocean.

Thirdly, they all agree that God is within us and cannot be realized anywhere outside. Guru Amar Das says: "Whoever seeketh Him without, findeth Him not, and is engaged in a wild goose chase. He wasteth his time and cometh to grief." Christ says: "The Kingdom of God is within you." "Seek thou the Lord there." The Quran declares: "Allah is near your royal vein." If we really wish to find Him, we have to seek Him within ourselves. He is close to us, but these physical eyes cannot see Him nor can our physical ears hear His Voice. Only when a seeker receives instructions from an Adept and learns to listen to the Divine Melody within, does he become capable of seeing and hearing Him.

Fourthly, all Saints assert that God can be realized only while we are in the human form. Neither animals nor angels, nor the denizens of the astral world enjoy this privilege.

Kabir says: "The gods yearn for a human incarnation, for the Lord is realized in this body alone." The gods yearn for the human form because devotion to the Lord cannot be practised in any other form, whether physical or astral. People imagine that gods are superior to human beings. The fact is that they are souls who performed virtuous deeds, such as charities, penances, etc., in their human lives (but did not devote themselves to the practice of Nam or Sound Current), and are consequently in Paradise, Swarg, etc., enjoying the fruits of their good actions. At the end of the prescribed period of reward, these devtas, gods, or angels will again be pushed down into this world. All the Saints and scriptures support this view.

Fifthly, the Saints point out that, within the body too, He is to be sought above the eyes, and not below them. Those who concentrate at any one of the lower centres such as the Mul Chakra (Rectal Centre), the Indri Chakra (Centre of Procreation), Nabhi Chakra (Navel Centre), Hirday Chakra (Heart Centre), or Kanth Chakra (Throat Centre), merely see the shadow. This is similar to beholding the reflection against a wall, of the sun's reflection in water, while the real sun itself shines above in the sky. Only one who has seen the real 'sun' above can testify that the reflection is that of the sun, and that it is merely the image and not the sun itself. Thus, only those who have seen the Lord within can realize that it is the shadow or reflection that pervades the lower centres and, in fact, the entire cosmos.

Now, the question arises, as to how to 'go within'? How to enter the palace of ten gates in which the soul dwells, and through which gate to go in? The answer is quite simple. Try to find someone who knows the secret of the 'house', who has himself been inside it and can take you 'within'. What do we do when we do not know the way to a place? We inquire from someone who knows the way. Likewise, before starting on our Spiritual Journey within, we have to seek the help of a Perfect Guide. Call Him Guru, Master, Friend, Teacher, Guide or Brother; the name makes no difference. Maulana Rum says: "If you intend to go for 'Haj' (Pilgrimage to Kaaba) take a 'Haji' (one who has already been there) with you, be he Hindu, Turk or Arab; look not to his colour or country. See whether he is familiar with all the ups and downs of the way." Again, he says: "Seek a guide, please. Without a guide the journey is beset with perils." And, again: "Who can conquer the mind without the help of a Master?" In his usual forceful way, Guru Arjan Dev says: "Let no one be deceived. None will cross the Ocean of the universe without a True Master, a Perfect Guide." Guru Ram Das also says: "With both my arms raised high, do I proclaim that none will realize the Lord without the help of a Master." Kabir Sahib says: "Go on counting your beads for years and give as much in charity as you like, but without the Guru all will be utterly futile so far as God-realization is concerned."

The Skand Puran says: "Guru is Brahma, Guru is Vishnu, Guru is Maheshwara. Guru is God himself. My obeisance to Him." For learning every science or profession, we have to seek the help of a teacher. That is the common experience. Then, would we not require a Teacher for the most difficult of all sciences, the Science of God and Spirit? Guru Amar Das says: "None will reach the Lord except through the Guru. This is ordained by the Lord Himself." You will have to obtain the secret of the

Inner Path and learn the technique from some True Master. "The key is in the hands of the Satguru. None else can open the door." (Guru Arjan). You can attune yourself to the Divine Melody only by acting in accordance with His direction. He will show you the way to 'go in' and contact Nam. Only then will you be liberated from the cycle of birth and death. "Those who do not go within and ever wander outside, simply waste this precious gift of a human life."

—*Guru Amar Das*

Now, the Path of the Saints is both simple and easy. From a child to an old man, irrespective of caste, creed, colour, and clime, all can easily follow the prescribed Spiritual Exercises. One is neither to change one's religion or mode of living, nor renounce the world and give up one's profession or business. Saints say: "Live in the world with your family, do all your duties, earn money honestly and spend it as you would a sacred trust, on your family and others who need your help. Live in the world but with a detached mind, all the while giving some time and thought to your most important duty of God-realization."

Dadu says: "Others speak only from hearsay. Saints see Him face to face." He cannot be approached by yoga, Pranayam, Mudra or Buddhi (intellectual reasoning). What should I say? How should I describe Him? He is not describable. Only Saints know what He is. The Path of the Saints is not that of Pranayam (control of the breath), yoga of the six chakras (meditation at the six lower centres), nor of Dhoti,* Neti, Vasti or Mudras. Saints do not waste the time of their disciples by starting them at the lower centres of the body. Besides, what does one get there?

The first or the lowest centre, the Mul Chakra, is presided over by Ganesh. The second, the Indri Chakra, is governed by

---

* See footnote on page 33.

Brahma, the creator of the bodies. The third or Nabhi Chakra is controlled by Vishnu, the nourisher or sustainer. The fourth, which is the Hirday or Heart Chakra, is ruled by Shiva, the destroyer. The fifth is the Kanth or Throat Chakra, presided over by the goddess Shakti, the source of power to the three gods Brahma, Vishnu and Shiva. The sixth Chakra, which is the highest stage reached by the yogis, is the 'Tisra Til' or the 'Third Eye', situated in the centre behind our two eyes, and is the 'Seat of our soul and mind', the 'Centre of consciousness', 'Thinking Centre.' This is the centre from where all our thoughts and energy go out. Our Creator, the Lord, is above in the twelfth chakra. Thus, we have to cross six more chakras above the seat of our soul, behind the eyes, to meet Him.

Would it be a wise step for us first to descend to the lowest chakra and then to commence the long and arduous journey upward from that lowest rung of the ladder? If you are in the middle of a hill and wish to reach its top, would it not be better to make your ascent from where you are rather than come down to the foot of the hill and then climb to the top? The latter would make your journey lengthy and tedious. But that is what the yogis do in their Spiritual journey.

And what does one gain by starting at the lower chakras? One meets only the deity or the power stationed at a particular chakra for the purpose of management of that particular function in the body (the microcosm). Moreover, this journey through the six chakras is so very difficult, hazardous and tedious that it is quite unsuited to the conditions of the present age. The 'Dharma' (method to be adopted) of each Yuga or Age is different. In this Kaliyuga, you cannot successfully adopt the yogic methods that were in vogue in the Sat or Treta Yugas, when life's span was longer and the struggle for existence negligible. The population was small and the land yielded all its requirements without much toil. Besides, men were strong, celibate and pure-minded. Would the young men of the modern age be able to carry through the hard exercises of Pranayam, Dhoti, Neti, Vasti and the difficult Asanas and Mudras? Even if they could, what a long time it would require! And where would that take us in the end? At its best, no farther than the eye centre. No, my friends, we are living in an age of automobiles and airplanes. We should not stick to the old methods of transportation.

The method of the Saints is Surat Shabd Yoga. The Muslim Saints call it 'Sultan-al-Azkar' (the King of Methods). It is the 'Anaahat Marg' of the Upanishads. This is the most natural and harmless method. You are not to renounce the world or become a 'Sanyasi', nor are you to change your mode of dress. It only calls for some time daily for carrying out meditation, while doing your other duties. It may be stressed that your primary duty is that of God-realization while in human form.

The Satguru will give you the technique at the time of Initiation. He will tell you how to 'go within' the Palace of Ten Doors, through the eye centre, by withdrawing your attention from the nine outlets and concentrating it at the 'Tisra Til', the 'Third eye', 'Shiv Netra' or the 'Nukta-i-Swaida'. Here the Heavenly Music resounds day and night. This melody comes direct from the home of the Lord. By attaching yourself to It, in accordance with the instructions of the Master, you will reach the Place whence It issues forth. This is the sum and substance of the Teachings of the Saints (Sant Mat). Only a fortunate few come in contact with a True Saint.

Surgeons who have dissected or operated on scores of bodies, have never found Brahmand or Sach Khand in any one of them. The answer is that they are not to be found by means of physicians' or scientists' instruments, nor can they be perceived by the gross physical senses. They are hidden behind the veil of the mind. Only when we become pure through spiritual practice and rend the veil of the mind in accordance with the instructions of a Master, can we realize the Lord. We have to dive deep into our own inner and real self, cross the intervening physical, astral, causal and pure spiritual regions, then reach the Highest Plane, the everlasting Sat Lok, to behold the Lord. Saints tell us the way and give us the technique which enables us to accomplish all this.

They teach us how to withdraw the mind and soul currents from the body, up to the eye centre, by concentrating our attention at the eye centre and contacting the Divine Melody, the Shabd, which is the Creator of all the regions and worlds, within and without. It is called by various names. Since we can hear It, It has been termed 'Shabd', 'The Audible Life Stream', 'The Sound Current'. This is the 'Word' or 'Logos' of the Holy Bible. In the Granth Sahib it is called 'Shabd Dhun', 'Nam'. It is the 'Kun' of the Quran, the 'Nad' of the Vedas, and the 'Anaahat' of the Upanishads. The Bible says:

> In the beginning was the Word, and the Word was with God, and the Word was God. The Same was in the beginning with God. All things were made by Him; and without Him was not anything made that was made.
>
> *–John* 1:1, 2,3

Soami Ji says: "Word created all the three worlds." In the words of Guru Amar Das: "The Word is responsible for creation and dissolution, and again creation comes into being through the Word." Guru Nanak says: "Word created the earth and sky. Word created all."

Word is the Creator, Preserver and Destroyer of all. It is called Shabd, Anhad, Anahat, Sat (True), Sehaj, Bani, Gur

Bani, Dhur ki Bani, Sachi Bani, Hukm and Amrit (Elixir or Ambrosia), in the Granth Sahib because he who partakes of It becomes immortal. Hindu Sages called it Ram Dhun, Akash Vani, Kirtan. Muslim Saints called it Baang, Sadai Asmani, Saut, etc.

The writings of the Saints always extol the glory of the Word or of the Master. Both are the same in Essence.

The Creator of the entire universe is One without a second. He is the Vital Force at the root of all activities.

Though He is the Creator of the Macrocosm as well as the Microcosm, He Himself resides within all. His search He initiated Himself, and Himself gave His own tidings. As He is Invisible, He always gives instructions through some human form. In fact, He Himself assumes the form of a Master and comes into the world to lift poor souls out of the misery and pain into which they have fallen. Through the link of the Word, He joins the seeker to Himself and thus bestows God-realization on the disciple.

The Supreme Being is within us. Nearest is He to us. His Throne is within us but we knock about outside in search of Him. God is far away only from those who do not 'go within'. Therefore, my friends, if you yearn for the Love of God, go to a Master and act according to His instructions in all earnestness. He will bring you face to face with the Lord.

We are all social beings and want the company of someone, be he a friend, relative or clansman. But true satisfaction comes only through contact with a Master. It is only He who can end our sorrows and sufferings by putting us in touch with the Supreme Being, the Source of all Peace and Bliss. God manifests Himself in the form of Saints in every Age. They come into this world and point the Way to the Supreme Lord. They are not attached to worldly objects as are the mundane people. They live in the world as a duck does in a pond; that is, it lives in water, eats and plays there all the day, but flies away with feathers quite dry. In the same way, Saints live in the world but are not soiled with its dross. Their soul ever remains with the Lord in all its actions.

No one knows when his end will come. Can anyone say when he will die? Death makes no distinction. It may come to a child, to a young person or to the aged. You have been incarnated in the human body as a result of past good deeds, but remember, this body will not last for ever. Therefore, make the most of it here and now. The eye centre is the 'Door' to the 'Palace of the Lord' in the body. Enter therein, listen to the Shabd, the Word, and awaken your love for the Supreme Being. Time will come when this body, this breath, this youth, will pass away. So, utilize the time to your best advantage before it is too late. Contact the living Master and attune yourself to the Voice of the Lord within, which calls you day and night. This is the message of the Saints.

Only the Word is true. All else is false. All the regions, the worlds and their kingdoms and rulers are perishable and subject to change. Thus, if you continue your attachment to the world, loving dross and perishable things all your life, you will remain confined to them in your next life. Therefore, detach yourself from the temporal things and attach yourself to the True Eternal Word.

Beware of the mind and its tricks. Those who obey the dictates of the mind flounder in the bog of illusion and never taste true happiness. There is no end to their misery. Evidence of it is found every day in letters received from persons who say that they are fed up with life and want to put an end to it. But this is a coward's approach. Death does not end their miseries by any means. Rather, they have to render further account for the act of taking their own life. The remedy lies within the human body. You will not find peace if you take your own life. If you love the Master, never, not even in a dream, let such a thought cross your mind. A person who takes his own life, goes straight to the lowest hell and suffers indescribable torment there. So, never think of committing suicide. If death were an escape from miseries, it would be a simple affair. But no, the miseries you will have to face hereafter would be out of proportion to the miseries here.

Guru Nanak says: "O Nanak, the entire world is unhappy. Only they find peace who live in Nam." Soami Ji says: "How tightly are we bound down by hoops of steel. The first bondage is that of our own body (instead of being universal, we become limited). The second is that of wife (because our attachments increase when we marry and have a family). The third is that of children, and the fourth of other relatives. As the chain lengthens, the bonds become stronger. Our own ailments and mental worries are additions, but those of our children and children's children lie heavy on our heads and present one long nightmare of pain and sorrow, strengthening our attachment to the world and resulting in our being born over and over again."

The basic principle is: "As ye desire, so shall ye reap." Nature must fulfil every desire of yours. If you attach your attention to Nam and strengthen that bond, you will not have to be reincarnated in this world. Those who are attached to the world must return to it to reap its pleasures and pains. While those who learn the secret of Nam from some Adept and get merged in Shabd, are liberated from the cycle of eight million, four hundred thousand species, the maze of life and death, and become one with the Supreme Being.

Plug the channels of lust, anger, greed, attachment, pride and egotism, all of which pull you down and draw you out. Man's attention has been scattered outside through these five passions since times immemorial. We have not yet found the

Path and have wasted our whole life in straying farther away from our Real Home. Only by attaching ourselves to and merging ourselves in something which is permanent and everlasting, do we become immortal; otherwise after death we are reborn in the form in which we can best fulfil our desires and thus once again go through the wheel of 'eighty-four.'

The soul itself is immortal, a Princess of Royal Blood, as it were. Its unhappiness lasts only so long as it is under the control of the mind. It is the company of the mind that has reduced it to the position of a 'slave girl'. Therefore, bring it under control of the Word, or the Shabd, to liberate it from the thraldom of the demon mind. Go within and connect your consciousness with Nam, so that you may be elevated out of this sphere of births and deaths. Thus will you achieve Eternal Salvation and Bliss.

To recapitulate :

1. Saints are those who have attained the highest stage and have become one with the Lord.

2. Saints alone are truly humble.

3. Their teachings are:

    (i)   The universe is not without a Creator, the Lord Supreme.

    (ii) The soul is in essence a drop from the Ocean of the Lord, but through long separation has completely forgotten its origin. This is the cause of all its misery and pain, which will end only when the drop again merges in the Ocean.

    (iii) God resides within and can be realized only in the human form.

    (iv) In the body, He is to be sought only above the eyes.

    (v)   None can realize God without the help of a perfect Adept.

4. Saints prescribe Surat Shabd Yoga wherein the attention, after being withdrawn from the body and concentrated at the eye centre, contacts the Divine Melody.

5. They also enjoin, 'Live in the world but be not of the world'.

6. Everything in the phenomenal world is unreal. He alone is Real and Everlasting. Go within, connect your consciousness with Nam and be liberated from the eternal wheel.

2

What is Guru Mat or the Way of the Masters?

Two paths are open to us in this world. Either we follow the path of the Mind, or that of the Guru, known as Guru Mat or Guru Marg. Everyone, according to his own light, claims to follow Guru Mat.

The Sikhs base this claim on the strength of the five symbols, referred to as the five Ks', which they wear: Kanga (comb), Kara (steel bracelet), Kachh (short knickers), Kesh (long hair) and Kirpan (sword). The five Ks are considered essential pre-requisites and without them none can claim to be a follower of their Guru.

The Muslims regard Namaz, Roza, Haj and Zakat (prayer, five times daily; fasting from sunrise to sundown for thirty days during the month of Ramzan, pilgrimage to Mecca, and giving a portion of their income to charity) as Guru Mat.

In the same manner, the Hindus regard Shikha (tuft of hair at the top of the head), Sutra (sacred thread), Sandhya (prayer both morning and evening), Havan (religious fire invoking gods) and Khat Karmas (six duties according to Hindu scriptures) as Guru's Way.

Some look upon idol worship, pilgrimages and baths in 'holy waters' as Guru Mat. Others take to reading the Gita, repetition of Gayatri, recitation of Ramayana or other sacred scriptures. And still others think that fasting and other austerities lead to God-realization. Yogis treat Pranayam (breath control) as well as Dhoti* Neti and Vasti Karmas as the path of God-realization. Christians, however, believe in Christ as the all-time Redeemer, with Baptism and the various sacraments, rites and rituals, as Guru Mat. In short, people do one thing or the other, and all claim to follow the Path of the Masters.

Let us now consider what is true Guru Mat? One makes progress according to the capacity and knowledge of one's Guru. But we find numerous gurus at every step. In fact, there are more so-called 'gurus' in this world than there are disciples. Kabir says "One's future depends upon one's Guru, and a Perfect Guru one gets only by rare good fortune." Since this world is full of 'gurus' of all sorts, how, then, can we find a true one? All the Saints and scriptures lay great stress upon finding a True, Perfect and Real Guru. In the Granth Sahib as well as in the writings of Kabir, Paltu, Dadu and other Saints, the need of a True Master is greatly stressed. Muslim Saints, such as Maulana Rum, Shams-i-Tabrez, Hafiz and others sing praises of Murshid-i-Kamil, the Persian name for a Perfect Master. Otherwise, there is the danger of the blind leading the blind and reaching nowhere. Consequently, the first requirement is to find a True and Perfect Master. The Perfect Masters always say: "The Kingdom of Heaven is within you." Lord God, the Supreme Creator, cannot be found outside by one who has not realized Him within. This human body of ours is the "Mansion of the Lord", the "Temple of the Living God." Those who seek Him outside, wander in illusion.

In the body too, the Lord is not realized in the Khat Chakras (six lower centres) as believed by the Yogis. He is to

---

* See footnote on page 33.

be realized above the eye centre, and the Way to realize Him is given by a True Master.

So long as the soul does not get out of the clutches of the mind and senses, and crosses the regions of Brahm and Par Brahm, Guru Mat is not really understood. The Guru initiates us into the mysteries of the Path and tells us how to vacate the body and enter the 'tenth gate' that leads to the Lord's Mansion.

Guru Mat is unique and sweet. It begins when the mind and the soul currents withdraw from the nine portals, according to the instructions of a Guru, and become concentrated at the "Bhru Madhe", the point between the two eyebrows. This is the door to the "Kingdom of Heaven within", about which Jesus Christ says: "Knock, and it shall be opened unto you." The Guru tells us that the way to knock at this gate is to totally withdraw the attention from the nine outlets of the body and focus it at the eye centre. By permitting the attention to function below the eye centre, we allow the mind and soul to run out, and squander precious energy.

When, by means of Spiritual Practice, soul and mind have reached the Asht Dal Kanwal (Eight Petalled Lotus), one begins to hear the Heavenly Music, called the Anahat Shabd (the Word or Logos of the Bible) which constantly resounds there. Thus the soul is attracted by the Voice of God, and its inward and upward flight begins. A new world of bliss is realized and vistas of the macrocosm open before it. By the Grace of the Master, it tastes the Amrit, the life-giving Nectar.

The soul that was previously burning with false and ephemeral desires of the world and of Maya, then begins to realize its true nature and to relish the Ambrosial Elixir of Nam, which bestows upon it true peace and bliss. The mind also, having for ages past, wandered from birth to birth, in the

whirligig of 'Chaurasi' (whirlpool of transmigration), becomes motionless. Then it begins to realize its own reality, its
high descent from Brahm. Thereafter it gives up the transitory
pleasures of the senses and experiences the everlasting bliss of
Celestial Music, the superior sweetness of which alone can
detach it from the lure of the world.

Formerly, it was as though the owner of the house (our
body) was asleep and the house was at the mercy of five
thieves, *viz:* lust, anger, greed, attachment and ego or pride
(ahankar). Now that the owner has woken up, the thieves have
run away. Huzur Baba Sawan Singh Maharaj Ji used to say
"when a soul 'wakes up', the five thieves go out and
inform the owner of the house that the place is now too hot
for them to survive there and they have to leave." Kabir also
said to annihilate the five perversions and be attached to
Nam. So long as the five enemies have control of the
house, the soul is a helpless prisoner. They leave it only
when the owner means business and will tolerate their
presence no longer. The Elixir of Shabd, which is the life-
giving Nectar for the soul, acts as a poison for these
thieves. They run away and the corresponding virtues take
their place. Thus lust goes and its place is taken up by continence,
anger is replaced by forgiveness, for avarice comes contentment,
and egotism and pride are replaced by discrimination and
humility. The mind, which hankered after trifles and whose
desire to possess knew no bounds, becomes still and contended.
The soul, becoming free from all entanglements, makes for its
real home. Holding on to the Melody of Nam, by the Grace of
the Master, it completes the journey of months in a matter of
days. The sense world now appears as an alien country, and the
regions inside as its native land.

As the Soul hears the sound of the Bell and the Conch, it
begins to drop off its impurities, and the lotus that lays

inverted turns right side up. The soul then travels up rapidly, and flashes of the distant Jyoti begin to come in view. The gate to Sahansdal Kanwal opens, whence the light and radiance from the Thousand Petals shines forth. This is the first stage on the Path of Guru Mat, but it is the highest and the last stage of several religions of the world. It is the seat of Niranjan, the Lord of the Astral world. The Yogis too go no further.

After the Thousand Petalled Lotus (the Sahansrar), comes the land of Brahm, Lord of the second Spiritual Region. He is the creator, the sustainer and the destroyer of the Universe. Connecting the two regions is an oblique passage,called the Bunk Nal (the Curved Tunnel). Only after crossing this tunnel, does the soul reach Trikuti, the realm of Brahm. Here the attributes of the mind drop off and thereafter the Soul ascends alone. Trikuti is the source of the mind. Once the mind reaches its Home, it merges in it thereby setting the soul free.

The soul, however has to sojourn in Trikuti for a fairly long duration of time. The store of Sinchit Karmas (the Reserve Store of Karmas) is located here, and the soul has to stay here until this store of Karmas is liquidated. Just as grain is separated from chaff, gravel and dust in a thresher, so is the soul purged of all its dross, while staying in this region.

Trikuti has three prominences, the highest being called the Guru Pad. It is a sublime stage, beyond description. As the python draws its prey towards itself, so does the Melody draw the soul towards it.

Next comes Daswan Dwar, the Region of Par Brahm. Here the music is that of Kingri, a stringed instrument similar to a guitar, which the Yogis generally keep with them and on which they play both morning and evening. Guru Amar Das refers to this Kingri when addressing the Yogis: "O Yogis, this Kingri of yours does not help in meditation. Play that Kingri which gives forth the Unstruck Music and draws the soul to the Supreme Being."

Now the Soul has transcended the Region of Potent Illusion. The tight knot which fastened It to the Mind has been cut asunder. All Its chains have been broken. The three coverings of physical, astral and causal bodies have been removed. The Soul now shines forth in the luster of Its full glory. Here it is that 'It knows Itself'. The true realization that It is not the body or the mind, but a spark from the Great Ocean of Light, Immortal and Eternal, comes to It on reaching this stage.

Shorn of all its fetters, the Soul now proceeds upwards and reaches the fourth stage called Bhanwar Gupha (The Whirling Cave). This is the gate to Sach Khand. But on the way between the third and the fourth stages falls the Maha Sunn (the Great Void), the land of Primordial Gloom. This is a region of utter darkness. Even though the soul has a refulgence of twelve suns, it is unable to penetrate this darkness by itself. And it is here that the soul realizes the greatness of the Guru, for by itself it is incapable of crossing this region of unfathomable gloom. Only a Sant Satguru, a Master having access to the highest regions, can take it through that darkness. It crosses this Timir Khand with the Guru's Radiance. The word 'Guru' in Sanskrit means "one who brings light to the darkness." Many souls, that did not have the good fortune of having a Perfect Master, remain lost in this darkness.

After crossing this Timir Khand, and on reaching the Cave, the soul sees that in essence it is the same as the Creator, the only difference being that it is a drop and He is the Ocean. This realization of its identity with the Lord of All Creation brings forth an involuntary cry from it: "I am He". (The Great Mansur was stoned to death by the ignorant Mullas for this cry

of "I am He" Ana-ul-Haq. What does poor intellect know of
the greatness of God-realization?)

From here the soul ascends to Sach Khand, the Sat Lok,
the True, the Immortal, the Eternal, the Home of Bliss and
perfect Peace, where there is no pain nor sorrow. This is the
Satguru Pad, the Abode of the True Master. Guru Arjan Dev
pays Him homage in the following terms at the commencement of Sukhmani.

> I bow to the Master, who was in the beginning;
> I bow to the Master, who was when time began;
> I bow to the Satguru, the True and Everlasting;
> I bow to the Gurdev, my Master, in human form.

There are no words with which the greatness, the
sublimity, the light or the extent of the Satguru Pad can be
described. Millions of suns pale into insignificance before the
effulgence of even one atom of this region. Guru Arjan says:
"By contacting the Shabd, we reach the Place where the light
of ten million suns shines and the gloom of delusion is
dispelled."

The music in Sat Lok is that of the Veena, a very fine,
stringed instrument. Guru Nanak says: "He who is attached to
the melody of Veena, knows the secret of the Three Worlds."
Namdev also says: " I will play on the Anhad Veena. Then I will
become Bairagi Rama–the Lord without any blemish &
attachment. Soami Ji says: "Wonderful is Guru Mat, where Mind
and Soul contact the Sound amid beautiful scenes inside."

From here the Sat Purush takes the soul to Radha Soami
Pad, after crossing the Alakh and Agam Lokas. This is the
Final Stage. Every Saint has referred to it as the 'Soami Pad.'
Guru Arjan Dev says: "My Exalted, Boundless, Infinite Soami!
Who can sing Thy praises (or know Thy worth)?" Kabir Sahib

says: "I bow to the Soami, the Beginning and the Creator of All." Soami Ji added the word 'Radha' (soul) to it, and addressed Him as 'Radha Soami', the Lord of the Soul.

Now you can judge for yourself how far and wide do people stray away from Reality. The Yogis and Gyanis have no knowledge of this. The Yogis, even after many years of hard labour in the Khat Chakras, could with great difficulty succeed in attaining the Sahansrar Chakra, the Thousand-Petalled Lotus. Yogishwars could only reach up to the top of the second region, Brahm Lok. As for the Gianis, the philosophers and the learned, most of them remained lost in hair-splitting. After facing failures, a few of them who sought the help of a spiritual guide, could go up to Brahm. This, again, brings home the necessity of a perfect Master because, no matter how hard one works, one cannot go beyond that stage to which one's Guru has access.

To recapitulate:

1. The first need in Guru Mat is a Perfect Guru.

2. From Him we learn the way to enter the tenth door of our body, the Temple of God.

3. We should make our entry through that gate which may take us direct to the Throne of the Lord, by the safest, shortest, easiest and most convenient way.

4. People who have not found a proper guide, have entered the wrong gate and wasted their lives in the labyrinth of the lower chakras.

5. Even the conquest of these chakras does not take us to the Highest Lord. Our births and deaths do not come to an end, and we find ourselves still in the maze of Chaurasi (the Wheel of Eighty-four).

6. We should make our ideal that Region which is Permanent and Eternal, whence we do not have to return to be born in this world. In Pralaya (Dissolution) all the regions up to Brahm are destroyed. In Maha Pralaya--Grand Dissolution--every thing up to the gate of Sat Lok *i.e.* all the regions below Sach Khand, come to an end. We should make Sat Lok our ideal, on reaching which we need never come down again.

7. Only the practice of Shabd, the True Nam, the Word, can take us to that Eternal Region.

8. All the pleasures of the world, the attachment to body and senses, the I-ness and duality have to be discarded before the Soul can become fit to partake of the sweetness of Nam. Only attachment to Shabd will detach us from the world and its objects.

3

The wonderful house in which we live

Have we ever given thought to our body? How wonderful is the twelve-storied house in which we live? What treasures lie hidden in it? What "gems of purest rays serene" this "dark, unfathomed cave" (the body) holds? The answer is generally in the negative. Is it not surprising that we have never cared to look inside the house in which we have been living for such a long time? We spend some time daily in looking after its outer cleanliness and appearance. In fact, some of us spend far too much time in trying to beautify "this muddy vesture of decay" and have never tried to find out what wonders lie hidden within. Thus we are absolutely ignorant of our possessing a mine of truly precious diamonds.

Guru Amar Das says:

In this cave lie inexhaustible treasures,
And the Infinite Creator too resideth therein.
In Some He keepeth Himself hidden.
And revealeth Himself in others.
(Those who kill their ego
By means of Guru's Shabd.)

Kabir says:

Within this muddy vessel (the body)
There are beautiful gardens

and the Gardener too;
There are gems and rubies,
    and their connoisseur
There are seven oceans, nine million stars
    and their Creator;
Within it also is our Master;
But what an utter darkness!
(That nobody sees them.)

Bulleh Shah, a Muslim Mystic, says:

When I learned the lesson of Love,
My mind rebelled against church and mosque.
I entered the real Temple of the Lord (the body)
Where a thousand instruments played.
I found my Beloved in my house.

This body of ours is the epitome of the universe, a microcosm
that holds the macrocosm within it. Hindu sages have called
it 'Nar Narayani Deh', the body that holds man and God within
it. Sikh Gurus have named it 'Har Mandir', God's Temple.
Guru Nanak says:

This body is the real Temple of God.

Christ refers to it as:

The Temple of the Living God

and says:

The kingdom of God is within you.

In fact, all the Saints and Sages who have made research in the
realms of soul and matter have come to the conclusion that our
body contains everything, namely, all that we see in this world
of phenomena as well as that which remains hidden in the
world beyond. They also claim that God can be realized only
within the body, and if anyone desires to visit the subtle, astral

and spiritual regions, he must search within himself. The Supreme Artist's real handiwork can only be seen within. Whatever exists outside is false. The reality of the body and of the entire macrocosm can be seen clearly and distinctly nowhere else except within ourselves. Guru Arjan Dev says:

> Within this house is everything;
> Nothing is without.
> Those who seek outside are in delusion.

Now let us make some research in the secret chambers of this house, about which Jesus Christ says:

> In my Father's house are many mansions.

Hindu Sages refer to this body of ours as a "house with nine doors." Sometimes it is referred to as a "house of ten gates." Nine gates open outward, through which our energies are dissipated. The tenth gate opens the Way to the Palace of the Lord within. The nine doors comprise our two eyes, two ears, two nostrils, the mouth and the two lower outlets. The tenth is in the centre behind the two eyes. It is called Tisra Til, Shiv Netra or the Third Eye. The Muslim Saints call it Nukta-i-Swaida.

A study of the inner structure of this house will reveal that it contains twelve stories, which can be divided into two parts. The part below the eyes is called 'Pinda'. It contains six chakras and extends up to the eyes. Above the eyes we have 'Anda' and 'Brahmanda' as well as the higher regions, which make up the second part.

Yogis enter the body from the lowest chakra called the Muladhar, and stop at the eye centre, which they consider the last and the highest region.

The Saints teach us to start from the eye centre, which is the headquarters of the mind and the soul in the waking state.

The Saints show us how to rise from this point up to Sat Lok, the fifth region above the eyes. They save their disciples the drudgery of going down and then treading the tedious, long, dreary and perilous maze of the Khat Chakras, Kanwals, Centres or Plexuses:

1.   The first Chakra, called *Muladhar*, is at the rectum. Its lord or ruling deity is Ganesh, the god with the elephant head. He is the lord of all the ridhis and sidhis. Those desirous of attaining this stage, concentrate their attention at this centre and repeat: 'Kilyang, Kilyang' ten million times. On reaching this stage the practitioner becomes the master of many sidhis and shaktis (miraculous and supernatural powers). His will power becomes so strong that if he orders a fast running train to stop it cannot move an inch further. This centre has four petals. Its colour is reddish. Prithvi (earth) is the dominant element (tattwa) here. It is the reflection of the four-petalled lotus behind the eye centre in the upper part. It is subject to change and dissolution. At the time of our death, when the current of our spirit begins to withdraw from the body, this is the first centre to be affected. During meditation, when our soul leaves the eye centre, we are dead to the world but fully conscious within. Our ideal is to attain eternal Liberation, to be one with the Immortal, Everlasting Lord of lords, Who is without beginning and without end and Whose Abode neither Pralaya nor Maha Pralaya can reach.

2.   The *Swadhishthan Chakra* is the genital centre. The lotus of this chakra has six petals. Its colour is whitish black, Water is the chief tattwa here and 'Onkar' is the word. Brahma (this should not be confused with Brahm, the presiding deity at Trikuti, which is the second Spiritual region and is in Brahmand, above the eye centre) and Savitri are the ruling deities of this centre. Their function is to mould physical bodies for the material world, in the same manner as a potter moulds

earthenware. This chakra is the reflection of the six-petalled lotus in Anda.

3. The *Mani Purak* is the third chakra and it is located at the navel ganglion. This chakra or lotus has eight petals. Vishnu and Lakshmi are the presiding deities. They are the nourishers and look after the maintenance of the body. Fire is the active tattwa, and its colour is light red. 'Hiryang' is the recitation of this place.

4. The *Hirday chakra*, the fourth centre has twelve petals and is located at the heart. It is the storehouse of the 'Pranas', the vital energy in the breath. Shiva resides here with his consort, Parbati. Their duty is the dissolution of life. Air is the ruling tattwa here and blue is the colour of this centre. The recitation at this place is 'Sohang'.

5. The *Kanth chakra,* which is a sixteen-petalled lotus, is the fifth centre and is located at the throat. The presiding deity is Ashtangi (the goddess with eight arms), the mother of the three lower gods, Brahma, Vishnu and Shiva, who derive their power from her. She is known by many other names, such as Shakti, Durga, etc. Darkish blue is the colour here, and Akash (ether) is the tattwa. 'Shiriyang' is the name repeated at this centre.

6. *Do Dal Kanwal* (two-petalled lotus) is the sixth centre, between the two eyes. It is called 'Shiv Netra', 'Tisra Til' or 'Third Eye'. This is the headquarters of our soul and mind during the waking state. From this point the currents of our soul have come down and spread throughout our whole body—in every cell and hair. This is as far as the Khat Chakras can take the soul. Pranayam cannot take one beyond this stage for the reason that the 'pranas', the energy in the breath, which form the vehicle used for ascent, merge in the Chidakash (sky within) at this stage.

Near the sacral plexus and associated with the function of

elimination is the 'Nadi' called 'Kundalini', which lies coiled like a serpent. This is the root of all the nadis. From it twenty-four smaller nadis spring forth, which support the body. Out of these ten carry the pranas to different parts of the body. Among these, Ida, Pingla and Sushmana are the major nadis, which control the breath. They reach only as far as the Shiv Netra, the Tisra Til, the Third Eye. The progress of those who follow Pranayam (the practice of rhythmic breathing), stops at Tisra Til, where these nadis end and the Pranas merge in Chidakash, the place of their origin. No power can carry one further than its origin. From here, some realize their limitation and take the help of the three canals or streams of the gunas* and manage to reach Sahans Dal Kanwal. This is the first chakra of Brahmand, whence the Way of the Saints begins.

The first chakra of Brahmand, called Sahansrar, has one thousand petals. From here, the management of the astral and the physical worlds is carried on. It is the seat of Niranjan, god of many religions.

Kabir Sahib has similarly given a detailed description of the various kanwals in his well known poem "Karnainondidar mahal men piara hai." He says, "See your beloved (the Lord) with your own eyes. He is within you. To do so, you will have to abstain from intoxicants and animal food as well as falsehood, lust, anger and avarice. Adopt, in their place, chastity, contentment, humility and forgiveness."

---

* The origin of which is in Trikuti

The practitioner of yoga should perform Dhoti[1], Neti[1] and Vasti[1] and, seated in Padam Asan[2], do Kumbhak[3] and Rechak[4].

The yogi is to concentrate first on the Mool chakra (ganglion). There the recitation should be Kilyang and the four-petalled lotus of red colour will be seen. God Ganesh is the Presiding Deity, and one gets innumerable supernatural and miraculous powers there.

Above that is the 'pleasure' centre which has a six-petalled lotus. God Brahma and goddess Savitri are the presiding deities. The recitation here is that of 'Onkar'. The procreation of the world is the function of this Deity.

Beyond this is the eight-petalled lotus at the navel, the centre of god Vishnu, attained by recitation of Hiryang.

It has from above the support of god Shiva and goddess Parbati, the presiding deities of the twelve-petalled lotus in the heart centre. The recitation here is 'Sohang.'

Above this is the goddess 'Avidya' in the throat centre seated on a sixteen-petalled lotus, which is attained by reciting 'Shiriyang.' From here Brahma, Vishnu and Shiva derive their powers. If the yogi goes up further, he will come to the two-petalled lotus behind the eyes. The mind rules from here.

Kabir says that he has described in detail the various ganglia which are all within this physical body. If, however,

---

1. *Dhoti* is a small piece of cloth, about 4" wide and the length is according to the capacity of the practitioner, which the yogis swallow and pull out through the mouth for cleansing the stomach. *Neti* is the cleansing of the humors by means of passing a waxed thread through the nostrils and bringing it out through the mouth. *Vasti* is a sort of enema, but the water is drawn up through the rectum by means of muscle control, while the practitioner sits in water.
2. *Padam Asan* is a sitting posture, cross-legged upon the ground.
3. *Kumbhak* is holding the breath in the lungs.
4. *Rechak*-is slowly exhaling it.

one wishes to realize the Endless, Deathless and the Everlasting
Supreme Lord (Satnam), one should contact a True Master and
listen to His satsang. He alone can guide the seeker within.

Shut your eyes, ears and mouth, and listen. By carrying out
His directions, hear the sweet melody of subtle Anaahat Shabd
(Sound) and behold the transcendent light.

By continuous practice, and under His guidance, you will
be able to cross the various stages above the eyes and realize
Him—the Supreme Lord of all.
Kabir says further that the centres within the physical
body below the eyes are mere reflections of the centres
above the eyes and are subject to dissolution.

Soami Ji says:

Of the physical body I describe the details of Lotuses, of
which there are twelve in all.

The first lotus is where Ganesh presideth.
In the second Immaculate Brahma resideth.
The third doth gleam with Vishnu's luminosity.
In the fourth are found both Shiva and Shakti.
Jiv-Atma[1] doth rule over the Lotus fifth.
While Parm-Atma hath sway over the sixth.
In the seventh lotus Kal hath his might.
He manifesteth there his spiritual light.
The eighth Lotus lieth in Trikuti,
Where sun of Brahm shineth forth brilliantly.
The ninth lotus taketh us to Daswan Dwar.
Par-Brahm liveth there quite afar.
Lotus 'Achinta' is found in Maha Sunn;
In the whole series it is the tenth one.
In 'Bhanwar-gupha' see thou Lotus eleventh.
And the twelfth glisteneth is Sach Khand.
The first six centres adorn the Pind,
The next three ornament Brahmand;

_____
1. Individual

The highest three nobody knoweth.
To these regions the saint alone goeth.
In the six centres do yogis sojourn,
Up to the ninth yogishwars have gone.
Pind and Brahmand do both end here.
Yogis and Gyanis no further go, dear.
None doth know the secret beyond.
The last three only the Saints adorn.
Some say six and others say nine,
And within these most faiths do pine.
Further than this only saints do lead,
The few that reach there are blest indeed.
He alone is the Saint Supreme,
Who can the twelfth centre redeem."

Now the only question to be decided is, which of the
twelve mansions should be selected as one's final objective?
At the time of pralaya (dissolution), the eight chakras up to
Brahm (the second in the upper six) are destroyed. All who
fail to cross the region of Brahm have to return and be born in
the world again. In fact, this is the case with all who have not
reached Sach Khand. Lord Krishna in Gita. (Chapter II,
stanza 45) says:

O Arjuna! The Vedas are concerned with the objects born of three gunas (they deal only with creation,
sustenance and dissolution of the world). Be thou above
these three gunas. Free thyself from the pairs of opposites, abide in Eternal Truth, detach thyself from worldly
possessions and become the master of thy mind.

Further on, in stanza 46, he says:

The value of the Vedas to a Brahman (an intelligent,
well-read person; the highest of the four castes; the

priestly class) is what a small pool of water would be to
one   who resideth with water all around him.

Similarly, all the regions below Sach Khand (eleven in
number) are effaced at the time of maha pralaya (Grand
Dissolution). Only Sach Khand, the Sat Lok is permanent,
eternal and deathless. Guru Nanak says: "Nirankar resides in
Sach Khand." This is the only region where dissolutions and
grand dissolutions do not reach.

Thus the human body has twelve chambers, divided into
two major parts—the Pind and the Brahmand--each containing
six chambers. The lower six are presided over by gods and
goddesses, whose function is to serve the soul in various
capacities. They are all subject to dissolution, although they
last longer than the material body. So, none of them is worthy
of being our Ideal or Goal. Only Sat Lok should be sought and
attained.

It may be necessary to point out here that Saints explain
the relative positions of various stages and regions along the
Path, and the functions of their ruling deities, not with the
intention of disparaging the teachings leading to the interme-
diary stages. In fact, the Saints never speak ill of anyone. They
are all Love and, they love all. But, as they come into this
world for the purpose of showing sincere seekers the way
back to their True Home, it is necessary that the relative
positions of different regions and their rulers be explained so
that the seeker may not be misled into thinking that one of the
regions, above this one but below the highest, is his True
Home.

Each region is so superior to everything below it that,
unless the seeker has been correctly informed, he will think it
to be the highest region and will have no desire to go further.

In that case he may become so engrossed in the pleasures of the region that he may get stuck up there until dissolution or even grand dissolution, depending upon the height of the region attained, overtakes him. Such persons will again have to go through the cycle of births and deaths, sometimes even in species lower than the human form, until they have again accumulated sufficient good karmas to receive the great gift of a human body. The Saints tell us that since it is only in human form that one can begin the real Spiritual Journey, why not start now?

On the other hand, if one knows beforehand that regions between this world and the highest are but stops on the way, he will not rest until he reaches his True Home of Eternal Peace and Happiness, from which he need never return. This duty lies heavily on the Saints and they have to perform it in a manner so as to enlighten the true seekers.

In singing the glory of Sach Khand as the highest Spiritual Region and in emphasizing the greatness of Sat Purush as the Highest Lord and Supreme Creator, their object is to give full and true information about the Lord.

Saints have no personal motive in making these statements. Their sole purpose is to shed light on the high status of the soul and its relation to the Supreme Being. Then we realize that there is no individual soul but that all is 'He' in various states of consciousness. We aim to reach the highest state, which is God-realization. We are now involved in duality, mine and thine, good and bad, and the like, but the Saints teach us how to rise above all this and realize our own highest state of consciousness. Thus, when they point out the stages and their rulers on the way, it is like showing us a road map that indicates the transit stops enroute to our Destination. Therefore, we should not be content to settle down until we reach our real Home. This is what the Saints tell us as clearly as it can be told in mortal language. In doing so, they are simply reminding us not to forget our Goal. Our body may be likened to a precious sandalwood forest, which we can exchange for millions of rupees (spiritual values) but we, in our ignorance, reduce it to charcoal in the fires of the five passions. The following anecdote aptly illustrates this point.

A poor old man lived in a forest and eked out his living by making charcoal from scraps of wood and selling it. One time, as a reward for rescuing a king who had lost his way in the forest, the poor man was given a beautiful grove full of the most fragrant type of sandalwood trees. These trees were of a special quality from which very expensive and rare perfume was made. One of these trees, in its natural state and without any effort on the part of the old man, alone was worth more than the poor man could have earned during the rest of his life by producing and selling wood as charcoal.

Of course, the poor old man was very happy over this gift, but did not realize what a great fortune was bestowed on him. So, in order to make a living, he resorted to making charcoal out of the sandalwood trees and selling it in the market for a pittance.

After a long time the king happened to pass that way again and noticed that the most valuable grove had been reduced to ashes, also that the old man was in the same poor condition as before. When the king inquired as to what had happened, the old man related that he had been earning his living by making charcoal from the trees. The king then asked him if he had any of the sandalwood left. The old man replied that he had nothing except a small piece, perhaps, one or two feet long. The king told him to go to the same bazar where he had been selling the charcoal and sell this piece of wood without first turning it into charcoal. There were some wealthy people in the bazar who noticed the excellent quality and rare fragrance of this piece of sandalwood. Recognizing its value, they all wanted to buy it. The result was that the old man earned hundreds of rupees out of that one small piece of sandalwood.

He returned to the king with the money, and the king said: "You have not appreciated the value of this wood. Had you appreciated it, you could have earned millions instead of the paltry sum you did by selling it as charcoal, and that too after going through the unnecessary labour of first making charcoal out of it." On realizing his mistake, the old man asked the king for another such gift that he might make proper use of it. The king replied that such a gift is bestowed only once in a lifetime.

In the same way, the true value of the human body is realized at the time of death, when man regrets that he has squandered his most precious possession. The result is that he has to go to hell or to lower births. Similarly, the Bible says that we are selling our birthright for a mess of pottage.

Thus we should choose that path which is safest, shortest, easiest and of highest reach. Such a Path is Surat Shabd Yoga. The Path through the lower chakras, you have seen, is so long, tedious and hazardous that it took the followers thousands of years of intense hard work to reach only up to Sahans Dal Kanwal. Moreover, that was the dharma (duty) of past yugas. In the first place, the span of life is not as long now as it was then; besides, who can now undergo the rigours and painful severity of those sadhanas (spiritual disciplines)?

The Path of the Saints is so easy that from a child to an old man—men, women, healthy or sick—all can follow it without trouble. You are not to change your religion or renounce the world, nor even alter your mode of living. There are no rites, rituals or ceremonies to be observed. Only you have to give two or three hours daily to your most important duty, which is devotion to God. A True Master will teach you the technique of Surat-Shabd Yoga, which enables you to hear the Voice of God.

To recapitulate :

1. The human body is a store-house of treasures and the temple of the living God.

2. This mansion has twelve stories which can be divided in two parts, six of which are in 'Pind' and extend up to the eyes, and the remaining six lie above the eyes in 'And' and 'Brahmand'.

3. During dissolution, eight of these stories up to Brahm are destroyed. In grand dissolution eleven of them are effaced. The lowest six (ganglia) are presided over by deities who depart before man's actual death.

4. Only Sach Khand or Satlok is permanent and eternal, and fit for our abode. All efforts should be directed to attaining this region.

5. The safest, shortest and easiest path is that of Surat-Shabd Yoga, and this can be learnt only from a perfect Adept.

6. The prerequisite is to give two to three hours daily to spiritual practices with love, faith and devotion. Thus we hear the voice of God, which alone can lead us to Deliverance.

4

NAM (The Name or Word) what it is and what it is not

People of all religions of the world—Hindus, Muslims, Sikhs, Christians, Jews and others—agree that Salvation is not possible without Nam. But the question is, what is Nam? Is it Ram, Rahim, Karim, Kesho, God or any of the hundreds of names that are prevalent in the world? A Hindu devotee says:

Hari[1] hath a thousand names,
Kesho[1] hath millions,
Bishen[1] hath a billion names,
And Madho[1] even trillions.

You must have heard Vishen Sahansar Nam (the thousand Names of God), which some of the Hindu devotees repeat every morning. Guru Gobind Singh has mentioned about twelve hundred names of God in his Jaap Sahib. But what is that Name without which there can be no Salvation? A Muslim Mystic begins his book with

To the Name of Him who Name hath none,
He surely answereth the call of any one.

---

1. Names of God.

That is quite true. The importance of that Power cannot be denied, but it makes no difference by what name you call it. If you call out the name of a sleeping person, he will instantly wake up and attend to your request. Would not He Who is ever awake listen to us if we call Him? He most certainly will respond, but we do not know the method of communicating with Him. Only a perfect Master can teach us how to gain His attention and hear His Voice. In fact, we do not know exactly what Saints mean by 'Nam'.

Paltu Sahib says:

'Nam', 'Nam' shouteth one and all,
But, none knoweth what Nam is.
For, Nam is distinct from all else,
Beyond description and beyond words.
He alone attaineth It who killeth all desires,
Obliterateth Ego and withdraweth
    from the body,
He siteth in the heart's chamber
    and drinketh deep of the cup of Love.
Oblivious of all hunger, and transformed in mind,
The Five[1] and Twenty-five[2] from him depart
From all burden is he freed.
In solitude he harkeneth to the Sweet Melody.
None can know it, Paltu, except one
    who hath heard.
It is through Guru's Grace
    and His Love benign
That he ascendeth into realms sublime.

---

1. The five passions of Lust, Anger, Greed, Attachment and Pride or Egotism.
2. The twenty-five Prakritis consisting of five Tattwas, viz., five attributes, each of five gross elements of ether, air, fire, water and earth are as below:
Ether: desires, anger, bashfulness, fear, infatuation.
Air: running, walking, smelling, contracting, expanding.
Fire: Hunger, thirst, sleep, personality, laziness.
Water: vital fluid, blood, fat, urine, saliva.
Earth: bones, flesh, skin, veins, hair.

This is the Nam, the Nad of the Upanishads, and Word of the Bible, which says:

> In the beginning was the Word, and the Word
> was with God, and the Word was God.
> The same was in the beginning with God.
> All things were made by Him; and without Him
> was not anything made that was made. In
> Him was life; and the life was the light of man.

—John 1:1, 2, 3, 4

Guru Arjan Dev says:

Regions and universes, subtle planes
And Nether worlds are created by Nam.
It giveth life and form to all.

Dariya Sahib says:

Dariya, seek thou the Guru (Master)
And beg of him to join thee with Nam.
This will give thee Gyan (Knowledge),
Cure all malady and lengthen thine life.
When the sun of Nam riseth in thee,
All darkness and delusion will doubtless flee.
Alas! very few reach the threshold of Nam;
Coming and going cease for those who contact it.

Gosain Tulsi Das, the famous poet Saint, in his great work called the Ramayana, says that Nam is greater than both Rama and Brahm. Rama was his ideal, his standard of perfection, in whose praise he had written the great Ramayana. He looked upon him as an Incarnation of the Supreme Lord. Yet he does not hesitate to say:

How can I sing adequately the glory of Nam?
When in this failed even Ram.

He continues:

Infinite, finite, God in forms two
(Sargun and Nirgun) is here;
Beyond words, beyond thought,
Without birth, without peer.
But greater than these is Nam, I dare say,
As both forms are gathered under its sway.

--Ramayana 1, 23

Then Tulsi Das shows how Nam is greater than Brahm
(the Infinite) and Rama (the finite):

Even though, the Immutable Brahm.
Doth dwell in every heart,
Yet every soul in this world is afflicted
And distraught till trying and pursuing, we attain Nam.

--Ramayana 1,23

Rama liberated a single woman,
The Sage's erring wife.
But Nam, numerous sinners hath brought
　to new life.
To faithful ones like Sabri
　and to vulture Jatayu
Rama gave in grace life immortal;
While Nam hath to countless vile sinners
　thrown open life's portals.
Well thou knowest how Sukant
　and Vibhishan doth Rama protect.
Yet Nam hath many more poor suppliants blest.

--Ramayana 1, 24, *Doha* 23

Naturally, the question arises in every seeker's mind, as to what that Nam is. Is it any word, syllable or sound? What is It that is given such supreme importance by the sages and Saints as to be called superior to God and Rama both? Clearly, it cannot be a word or a collection of words. Words and syllables cannot create universes or give life to dead matter. Guru Angad Dev says that Nam is neither spoken by the tongue nor seen with the eyes nor heard with the ears:

> Seeing without eyes, hearing without ears,
> Walking without feet, working without hands,
> By realizing His Order, Oh Nanak,
> We are united with the Lord.

This 'Order' (Hukum), is the Word, the Logos, the Nam.

One may doubt how Sound can create and maintain the universe. This is not the subject of intellect or reasoning. Reasoning takes us only to a certain point. Beyond that we have to take the help of anubhav (inner experience) and till we have developed the power of comprehension without reasoning, we have to depend upon the experiences of those who have gone within and have seen with their own eyes. In the meantime, faith must replace reason.

Now we come to the question, as to how to get this intuition and the subsequent inner experience, or how to get Initiated into the Mysteries of Nam, the Word. For this purpose, we have to seek 'One who knows.' We have to go to a perfect Master.

Guru Amar Das says:

> Nam can be had only from a True Guru.
> Without Nam the world could not exist.

Real Nam is Shabd. Soami Ji says:

Nam is the support and sustenance of all.
The wonderful treasure of Nam
  is in the heart of the Saints.
And only from them can we obtain
  this precious wealth.

But no, the mind, our deadly foe, does not allow us to take this course. It beguiles us into strange practices for God-realization. Some go to temples and mosques; some to places of pilgrimage; some take recourse to baths in holy tanks and rivers; some worship idols and deities; some give themselves to study of scriptures; the educated lose their way in the labyrinth of learning. None, however, can realize Him by these means. The Lord is inside, but the world seeks Him without. It is the same as the old story of a fond mother who proclaimed the loss of her child throughout the village when it was in her own arms all the time.

The more zealous take to yagña (sacrifices), tap (austerities) and dan (charities), or to ashtang yoga. But they miss the essential point. The law of every yuga or age is different. The methods and ways of attaining God-realization are, therefore, not the same in every age. Their toils and labours are thus in vain, like that of the ignorant farmer who sows the seed out of season. In the present age, all actions and practices, apart from Nam, are like sowing seed out of season.

Guru Arjan Dev says:

Kalyug hath come; sow the seed of Nam.
This is not the season for other practices.

The laws of past yugas are not applicable to the present age. what is the law of the present age? Guru Nanak says:

> In Kalyug, Kirtan (the Song, the practice of Shabd)
>   is supreme.

Soami Ji says:

> Except for Shabd, there is no other way
>   to get out of this cage of the body.

This Shabd practice can be learned only from a perfect Master.

Paltu Sahib says:

> Dear to Saints is Nam,
> And so doth Nam love saints.
> Only They can attach us to it,
> As they possess full knowledge thereof.
> With no amount of recitals, austerities,
>   pilgrimages and fastings,
> Nor ceremonies, rites nor rituals
>   can anyone achieve success,
> For it is the Saints alone
> Who can bestow the gift of Nam.

Saints say that Nam is of two kinds, Varnatmak and Dhunatmak. Varnatmak Nam is that which can be spoken and written, as are the languages of the world. It is of four kinds:

1. *Baikhri* (oral)–that which is spoken with tongue and lips.
2. *Madhyama* (silent)–that which is repeated silently in the throat.
3. *Pashyanti* –that which is repeated in the heart.
4. *Para*–the current or wave which the yogis raise from the navel.

People throughout the whole world make use of Varnat-mak Nam. There are many such names and they differ with different people, races and countries. Religious books and scriptures are full of them. These names, however, cannot liberate the soul from bondage. The Name that does so is common to all. The latter recognizes no caste, creed, colour, race or nation. It resounds in every human being. It is not the design of any man. It is natural, without beginning or end, and was created by God Himself. Before the creation of the world It was. It is called Dhunatmak Nam. Vedas and Upanishads call It Nad, Akash Vani, Anaahat Shabd. It is also called Hukum, Sound, Sound Current, Audible Life Stream, Shabd, Anhad Shabd, Anaahat Nad, Dhun, Akash Bani, Dhur-ki-Bani, Sachi-Bani, Gur-ki-Bani, Sach, Sehaj, Ram Dhun, Ram Nam, Arti, Keertan, etc., etc. Different Saints of different countries and ages have given It different names. Muslim Saints have called it Kalma, Baang, Nada-i-Asmani, Saut, Ism-i-Azam (the Highest name), Avaz-i-Khuda (the Voice of God), Sultan-al-Azkar (the King of Names), Kalam, etc. Christ called it Word or Logos.

Dhunyatmak Nam has nothing to do with the physical body. It can neither be spoken, written or seen, nor can it be perceived by other senses. Only the soul can comprehend it and that too when a perfect Master shows us how to attach our soul to it.

The difference between the two, Varnatmak and Dhunyatmak Nam, can be appreciated only when, by the Grace of a perfect Master, one goes within and concentrates his attention at the centre where the Dhunyatmak Nam, the Celestial Sound, the Voice of God, the Word, resounds. Then it will be clear that one is the spoken word and the other is the Nam itself. Varnatmak Nam is necessary for purifying the mind. When the gross impurities are removed, the mind and the soul begin to relish the sweet taste of Dhun and are lifted upward and inward. Then the subtle impurities are removed stage by stage. Varnatmak Nam is the means, while Dhunyatmak Nam is the end and object.

True Nam cannot be realized below the eyes. One's attention has to be withdrawn from the Pinda; in other words, it has to quit the nine portals of the body (two eyes, two ears, two nostrils, the mouth and the two lower apertures) before one is able to attain Nam. This is called 'dying before death' by the Muslim Saints, and is what St. Paul meant when he said 'I die daily'. When the soul, leaving the nine portals, enters the tenth gate during life, it hears the heavenly Sound (the Nam) which is resounding behind the eyes in the Tisra Til. The Voice of God beckons us there all the times but we do not hear Him until our attention is concentrated at the proper centre. As soon as one concentrates attention in the Sushmana, one begins to hear the Sound. This is the Nam or the Word. It is neither in Sanskrit, nor in Arabic, nor in Persian, nor in any other language. It is the language of God, which each and every one can understand.

All Mahatmas of higher order, to whatever country or religion they belonged, have followed this Path. This was the Way of Guru Nanak, Kabir, Maulana Rum, Shams-i-Tabrez and all the other Saints.

Guru Amar Das says:

Close the nine doors
And stop thy mind from wandering,
Enter thou the tenth that leads thee
To the Eternal Home.
There the sweet melody resounds
    day and night.

Attain thou this with the guidance
of a Guru.

Maulana Rum says:

Shut thine eyes, ears and lips.
If then thou find not the Secret
Of God, scoff at me.

When questioned by Rukan-ud-Din of Mecca, Guru
Nanak said:

High above in the Lord's Mansion (our body)
Ringeth the transcendent music.
But, alas, the unlucky hear Him not;
They are in deep slumber.

About the oral recitation of Nam, Guru Nanak says:

Read thou every year
And every month thereof;
Read thou throughout life
And with thy every breath;
O, Nanak! Save Nam all else is false and vain.

Maulana Rum says:

Thou art reciting the Name;
Seek the Name One.
The Name without the Named One
Is of no avail.

Another Saint says:

What doth it avail thee if thou utterest
His Name but hath seen Him not,

Nor hast thou touched Him.
If mere talk of wealth could make men rich,
Then none would remain poor.

The Treasure of Nam is within us, but the key to It is in the hands of the Guru. Brahmand and Sach Khand are within, but none can reach there without the Master's help. Two things are essential:

1.   The perfect Master, and full faith in Him, and
2.   Hard and earnest effort on the part of the disciple to practise Nam.

Like all other wealth, one gets this wealth also as a result of hard labour. It demands a great sacrifice. You cannot get it by mere talking. However, one is not to renounce the world or live in seclusion in a forest or a mountain for this purpose. Saints enjoin:

Live thou in the world, but be not of the world.
Do thy duty towards thy family and others;
Carry on thy profession yet do no fail
     to attend regularly to God's devotion
Give at least three hours daily to meditation.

The main object, and purpose of human life is to attain God-realization. Guru Arjan says:

Many lives hast thou passed
     as insects and moths,
Many as elephants, fish and deer;
For many lives wert thou bird and serpent,
And for many horse and tree.
Oh seek God now,
This is the time of union with the Lord

For after a long time hast thou got
the human form.

Family, parents, children, we had in every life. Food,
sleep, lust and greed are also common to all forms. The
unique quality in human life, which is not present in other
forms is the capacity for God-realization and permanent
release from the prison-house of Chaurasi. This rare privilege
is not bestowed upon any other species. This is the time to seek
a Master, learn the technique from Him and reach our Eternal
Home, whence we do not return to this world again.

Saints come in the world to help us in this task. They do
not exclude even the thieves, robbers or criminals from their
mission. They love all beings, including the birds and the
beasts. Just as a washerman does not refuse to wash any
clothes, howsoever greasy and dirty they may be, knowing
that if not the first, the second washing will doubtless cleanse
them, so also the Saints do not turn away even the vilest of
sinners, but willingly take them under their protection. They
see the purity of the soul under the coverings of filth. The filth
of the sins is removed when we follow the instructions of
the Saints. The Saints give the message of Surat Shabd Yoga,
the practice of the Holy Sound, the Word. The sage who is not
a practitioner of Shabd is not a perfect Master. The latter
takes the disciple right up to the Fifth Stage within. He gives
us the Names of these five regions and describes in detail the
lights, sounds, music and other attributes. Thus a true Saint
takes His disciples through Sahansrar and Brahm, up to Sach
Khand, the Eternal Region of Bliss, which is not subject to
dissolution and change.

The first essential worth imbibing is that the object of
Nam is and should be only God-realization and return to our
Original Home. Nam should not be misused for either earning

wealth or gaining worldly fame. People often run after supernatural powers and cannot resist the temptation of using them when they acquire them. *Sidhis*[1] and *Shaktis*[1] automatically come to a disciple, but he should pay no heed to them, because these are the devices of Kal (negative power) to keep the souls within his domain. Maharaj Baba Sawan Singh Ji frequently warned his devotees against the use of these powers. He likened such use to the squandering of hard earned wealth in despicable pursuits.

This body is a veritable mine of everything precious and occult. But a true seeker is enjoined to steadfastly pursue the task of union with the Lord, avoiding the pitfalls and temptations that beset this path. Thus shall he achieve his objective.

The second essential to remember is that so long as the seeker does not attach himself to Nam (the Audible Life Stream), he remains subject to egotism (I-ness) and the consequent misery and bondage. Even good actions like charities, penances, austerities, etc., cannot take him out of the cycle of transmigration. The good actions performed with a desire for reward are like golden chains, while bad ones resemble iron fetters. Both, however, keep us confined to the prison house of life and death.

It is thus the choice of the seeker whether to remain confined within the nine sense apertures, or to seek guidance from an Adept in raising his consciousness above them and connecting it with the Sound Current (Nam), which alone can take him out of this prison. This, however, requires concerted and sustained effort in the practice of Nam. If only we were to give as much time to our spiritual practice as we do to worldly pursuits, we would doubtless attain liberation.

---

1. Miraculous and Supernatural Powers.

The tragedy is that we do not run away from sensual pleasures, nor are we afraid of offending Him even though we are told daily of the presence of Nam, the Supreme Being within us. We would not dare commit an evil act in the presence of a small child, yet what wicked sins do we not perpetrate in His Omnipresence? Evidently, we do not fear God as much as we do even a child. Unless the mind develops awe for the Lord, success can hardly be expected. Love and fear go hand in hand, and both are essential prerequisites to a lasting attachment.

To recapitulate:

1. No one is happy in this world of phenomena.

2. True happiness will come only when we give up attachment for this world, concentrate our attention at the eye centre according to the directions of the Guru and return to our Original Home where prevail perfect Peace and Bliss. This is possible only in the human form.

3. God-realization, that is, return to our Original Home, is not possible without Nam.

4. Nam can be obtained only from a True Master.

5. This Nam is unspoken and unwritten, and cannot be perceived by the senses.

6. It is within our body, where it rings constantly as a sweet Melody, but can be perceived by the soul alone.

7. Even in the body, It can be realized only when we concentrate the attention at the eye centre.

8. Our aim is to reach that Region of Bliss which is beyond birth and death and is Eternal.

9. Austerities, charities, pilgrimages and other similar acts, though they may be good and virtuous, do not take us

out of the cycle of transmigration. We have to be reborn again into this world to enjoy the fruits of these actions.

10. Only the Nam, the Shabd, the Sweet Celestial Melody that issues forth from the feet of the Lord's Throne can take us to the place whence It comes. And that too only if we follow the instructions of the perfect Master.

11. This can be done only in human form. If we miss the opportunity, we go down into an abysmal dungeon of births and deaths.

out of the cycle of transmigration. We have to be reborn again into this world to enjoy the fruits of these actions.

10. Only the Nam, the Sabd, the Sweet Celestial Melody that issues forth from the feet of the Lord's Throne can take us to the place whence it comes. And that too only if we follow the instructions of the perfect Master.

11. This can be done only in human form, if we miss the opportunity, we go down into an abysmal dungeon of births and deaths.

5

Downfall of the Soul and how it can return home

Our soul is, in essence, a drop from the Great Ocean of Sat Nam—the True, Eternal, Inconceivable Lord, without beginning and without end, the Creator of all. He is the Source of all Bliss, Energy and Life.

After departing from their source, Sat Nam, the souls of the entire universe descended into the domain of the mind. Then they were confined in the prison-house of the world through the bondage of their desires. They lost awareness of their Sire, Sat Nam, and forgot their Divine Origin. Whatever actions the soul performed at the bidding of the mind, involved it more and more in the worldly dross. It became tied down here, to the earth plane, and its desires and cravings became its fetters. The further it strayed from its Home, the darker and dirtier coverings it acquired.

The soul was then submerged in duality, which resulted in its encasement in a thick, hard shell of egotism. So its light became clouded by mental aberrations and desires. Treading the path of mind, it strayed further away from the path of Nam till, at last, all its light and glory got totally masked. It even forgot that it was 'soul'—Immortal and Everlasting—and began to identify itself with its various coverings, with which it had enveloped itself during its descent. It began to call itself 'body'. First, it took on the causal body, after descending to the Causal Region. When it came down to the Astral Region, which is the world of potent illusion, it was covered with the astral body. And when it dropped down to the phenomenal world, it was covered with the physical body, in addition to all the previous coverings. The lower the soul sank, the dimmer grew its light.

Consequently, whatever we do in this world, our actions are like those of a blind man groping in the dark. The darkness and ignorance result in confused thinking which, in its turn, brings sorrow and suffering. The mind is weak and erring, and is the victim of the senses. As the soul is practically tied into a knot with the mind, it has also to undergo the sufferings of the latter.

You will find no dearth of misery and suffering in this world. Ask anybody, whether rich or poor, prince or pauper, man, woman or child, young or old, and you will find that no one is happy. Guru Nanak says:

> Unhappy is all the world, Oh Nanak,
> Happy are those devoted to Nam.

Sahjo Bai says:

> The rich, without exception,
>   are distressed and distraught.
> And the poor, what to say of their lot ?
> Their misery and sorrow know no bound.
> Blessed are Sadhus who the great secret
>   have found.

Soami Ji describes the misery of man, from birth to death, in the following words:

> As a baby, immense pain he suffers.
> Neither makes he a sign, nor a word utters.

He cannot tell what ails him.
In pain, he weeps and cries;
But parents are at loss to understand
    the cause.

He suffers from one disease,
But is treated for another.
This adds more to his trouble;
Thus babyhood passes in great distress.

Then he enters boyhood.
Parents want to send him to school;
But he has a burning desire for play
    and games.
Gets daily thrashed, nobody saves him.
What a pity ! What great pains !
These days also passed in vain.

Now cometh youth, the age of folly.
Lust and passions awake in mind.
Desire driven, he runs after woman;
Marries and brings home his bride.
Her company he enjoys,
Knoweth not that he is chained.
He forgets altogether parents' rights
Day and night he dallies with wife.
When children appear,
Love for parents doth disappear.

Next worries for livelihood come.
He runs from door to door;
Like a dog he gets rebuffs.
From morning till evening,
Of nothing else he thinks;

Money is his prayer and money is his king.
Wants and worries do increase,
Make hell of life and bring disease.

Maintaining position and pride of caste,
All these burdens he takes to heart.
What a fool, to load his head with grief.

He gets perplexed and runs in search of peace;
But instead he gets sorrow and pain
Regrets his folly, but to no avail;
Misery and distress come like rain.
Now that the rainy month has started.

Such is human life, which is regarded as the top of all creation. Even worse is the condition of the lower species. Every day thousands of fowl, sheep, goats, cattle and other animals are killed to provide food for man. Piteous are their agonising cries, yet we heed them not. Never have we thought for a moment how we would feel if we were in their place, waiting to be butchered. A slight prick of a doctor's needle is enough to frighten us and to make us shiver, even though it is for our benefit. How oblivious are we of the pain we cause to animals when we go hunting! How the birds flutter and scream when they are shot! How the wounded animals suffer torture and slow death! How the poor fish writhes and wriggles in trying to save its life when it is caught on the angler's hook and is pulled out of water! Witness the fate of mules and horses. The vehicles pulled by them are infrequently loaded much above capacity. They are made to run despite the bad and uneven roads. Lashes fall on them mercilessly even though they have sore necks and backs. When they grow old and are unable to do work, they have either to fend for themselves or suffer the butcher's knife. To whom can they complain?

You will find that, in all the bodies and in all the species, the soul has indeed a hard lot to face. Misery and pain surround it wherever it goes. To what a sad plight the association with the mind and senses has brought it! A princess of royal blood who would normally marry a ruling prince and rule as a queen, has completely forgotten her high origin and has run away with a lowly slave who makes her do menial work. Possessing her and getting work done, however, does not satisfy him and he continually runs after others (in the garb of senses).

The above aptly illustrates the position of the soul. This Royal Princess has fallen into the hands of the mind, which has brought nothing but misery and pain to her. The mind itself is not free. It runs after the pleasures of the senses and has become a slave to lust, anger, greed, attachment and pride. The mind and the soul have become so tightly knotted together that the soul has to suffer the consequences of the mind's actions. It keeps moving from one species to another, each one worse than the former. The only exit from this prison was the human form, of which it did not avail itself. The purpose of the Supreme Being in blessing the soul with the most valuable gift of a human body was to afford it an opportunity of release from this vast prison-house by devotion to God. But this poor wretch utterly failed to take advantage of the golden opportunity. Instead, he resorted to eating, drinking and gratifying lust, greed, etc. This reminds us of a popular adage: "Sweet is this world, who has seen the next?"

Nature is not extravagant. If the soul does not make proper use of its vehicle, it is consigned to the place where it can satisfy its desires and cravings. The result is that the soul descends lower and lower till ultimately it sinks to the lowest hell. Man stands at the highest rung of the evolutionary ladder.

By carrying out the instructions of a perfect Master, he can gain the rooftop—his real Home in Satlok. He follows, however, the dictates of his mind and senses, and suffers the consequences thereof by falling down in the scale of evolution. It may take him countless ages to be born again in the human form.

This continuous chain of action and reaction would never have come to an end, had not the Supreme Lord taken great pity on us in our extreme distress and misfortune. Seeing the soul, His beloved child, in such a sad plight, that Ocean of Mercy and Compassion surged in swelling tides and, assuming the human form, came to the world to save us.

Soami Ji says :

> The Lord assumed the human form,
> Came into the world in Master's garb,
> To awaken the souls from deep sleep.

When an erring son is arrested by the police and sent to jail for crimes, it is the father who runs about, files an appeal and follows the case up to the highest court. However angry he may be over the evil doings of his son, he does not forsake him in time of need. When such is the case with a father who has nothing but physical attachment to move his heart, would not the Almighty Father Who is the Unfathomable Ocean of Mercy, Grace and Compassion take pity on us and come to our rescue? All the Saints say "He will and does come."

Kabir Sahib has said:

> Father, Merciful and Kind, forgive my faults,
> Though unworthy, still thy son am I
> And dependent on Thee! Oh Father.

Shamas-i-Tabriz says:

> That Great Lord has hid Himself
>   behind heavy palls
> Then concealed in the cloak of man,
> Cometh He to (open) the door.

Further he says:

> Sit silently in a quiet corner
> And listen to the five notes
> That constantly arise from within thee.
>
> Oh, hush thee and listen thou
> To the five Melodies coming from Heaven.

Bulleh Shah says:

> God cometh in the form of man,
> And cometh He to awaken the world.

Guru Arjan Dev says:

> Hari[1] has assumed the name of Ram Das. [2]

God has to assume the human form for our sake, because only a human being can teach a human being. Gods and angels we cannot see; animals and beasts are without understanding or the faculty of speech. Only a human being can make a human being understand. Krishna, Kabir, Christ, Mohammed, Guru Nanak, Soami Ji and all the Saints and Sages, Rishis and

---

1.   God.
2.   Ram Das was the name of the Guru of Arjan Dev.

Munis that visited the earth came in the human form. When the Great Lord wishes to impart Gyan (knowledge about Himself) to us, He always comes in the human form. Had He come in any other form, we would not have understood His language. Moreover, there is natural attachment and attraction towards one of the same species. Had not the Great Lord come Himself and apprised us, we would never have known anything about Him. Out of compassion, grace and mercy, does He take the human form and come down to this world as a Teacher or Guru. He is not confined to any particular race, religion or country. All races and countries are His.

Saints, who are men of God and whom we call Gurus, Teachers or Masters, are above caste, colour and creed. They have nothing to do with the worldly ceremonies, symbols, forms, rites, rituals or religions. They belong to all religions, and all religions are Theirs. They simply say:

> Brothers! This world, full of misery and pain, is not thy true Home. Thou belongest to the land of Everlasting Peace and Bliss, where there is no grief, disease or death. These religions are not thy religions, nor are these castes thy castes. Thy religion is love. Thy caste is Sat Nam. Thy country is Satlok or Sach Khand. Thou art the son of the Father, the True, Eternal, Unborn, Deathless, without Beginning and without End. Thou hast fallen into the hands of Mind and Maya, who have kept thee confined to the wheel of births and deaths. Human form is the only exit through which thou canst find escape.

Kabir says:

O Swan (soul)! Proceed thou to Sach Khand.
And quit thou this foreign land
  (where there is no peace).

Soami Ji says:

Return thou to thy own true Home;
Stay not in a foreign land.
Do thine own work,
Engage not in others.
Devote thyself to the practice of Nam,
Which alone shall in good stead stand.

All the Saints have expressed similar sentiments.
Maulana Rum says :

This world is a prison
And we are all prisoners in it.
Break through the roof of thy cell.
And release thyself.

Our soul is 'Maha Chetan' (superconscious energy), a drop from the Ocean of Spirituality, Life and Energy. It is pure spirit. Yet in its association with mind and matter it has gathered all the dross, which is the cause of recurring woe and misery.

The soul is in search of peace and happiness. It tries to find it sometimes in one thing and sometimes in another. But where can it find peace in this phenomenal world, where none is happy? Everyone has his own tale of woe to narrate. One has a wife and the other none, but both suffer all the same. One has no children and the other too many. One is worried about realization of a loan, the other about his inability to pay. One bemoans the loss of a son and the other his son's misdoings. Poverty, disease, and suffering stalk the land. Rich and poor, king and beggar, young and old—all are restless. The world is literally a Pandora's box—a home of misfortune. True happiness does not exist anywhere. Neither wealth nor pelf can buy it. Mr. Rockefeller, the world's richest man of the time once remarked on seeing a labourer carrying a heavy load, "Take all my wealth and give me the health of that man." Even when one is seemingly happy, one carries a heavy load of cares on one's head. The moments of joy are fleeting and soon pass away only to be followed by bitter grief and dismay.

Guru Nanak says:

Too much enjoyment resulteth in pain,
Indulgence in normal pleasures
Endeth in disease and dejection.
Pleasure removeth not pain,
And in delusion doth man come and go.

The pleasure which ends in pain is not real pleasure. Wise men always keep the end in view. In short, the Saints say that this is not our True Home. It has nothing to offer but pain and sorrow. Quit this place as soon as possible and reach your True Home in Sat Lok without delay. Take heed! This work can be accomplished only in the human form. Therefore, take full advantage of this opportunity, for it is the greatest good fortune to be born as a human being after long and tortuous wanderings in other lives. You have a short span of life and this too is running out fast. Unless you wake up now, it will be futile to cry over spilt milk later.

Guru Arjan Dev says:

Having reached the top of the evolutionary ladder, you should now contact Nam and tread the Spiritual Path to your Divine Home. If you fail to do so and
slide down, you will have to sojourn in this world of
change and go through the various forms of creation.

Kabir Sahib says:

Human body is hard to obtain.
One doth not get it again and again.
When a ripe fruit once falleth from a tree,
Never again doth it return to the branch.

Soami Ji says:

This valuable body you got
After roaming in millions of lower lives.
Now do not lose it in vain pursuits.
Take heed! Give your attention to Devotion.
Have pity on your poor soul
And save it from transmigration's wheel.
These pleasures and comforts are for four days.
After that a long period of sorrow awaits you.
Beware! save yourself from hell-fire;
Do not make your soul its fuel.

Saints loudly and repeatedly enjoin:

Turn away from the path of sensual pleasures. God
is within your body. Seek the True Master and learn from
Him the way to go in. Raise your consciousness above
the nine portals and attach yourself to Nam, the Heavenly
Sound, the Voice of the Lord that is resounding behind
your eyes. Concentrate your attention on the akash (sky)
within, and go up from there to higher regions.

We have been turned out of this 'mansion' and an iron
gate has been shut against us. This can be opened only with the
help of a perfect Guru. It is impossible to undertake the
journey inside without a Perfect Guide—One who knows all
the 'ins and outs' and 'ups and downs' of the dark passage. At
every step, there are obstacles and hindrances which make it

difficult and dangerous for the practitioner to proceed alone.

Maulana Rum says:

Find thou a mystic guide,
For beset with dangers is this journey.
Whosoever without the Master
   ventureth on the path,
The 'evil ones' lead him astray,
And cast him into the well (of misery).

If over thy head the protecting hand
Of thy Guru thou hast not got,
Devilish doubts shall ever keep thee
Perplexed and puzzled.
Many, wiser than thyself, tried to go
On this path
But Satan led all of them astray.

When good luck brings you in contact with a True
Master, offer all your love to Him. Give up attachment to the
world and the worldly objects, and discard the path of mind
and senses. Take the Master with you and enter inside. He will
attach you to Shabd. Identify yourself with It and become one
with It. By and by, you will be able to withdraw your
consciousness, first up to the ankles and wrists, then to the
knees and elbows, thence up to the shoulders, and so on. Do
not lose heart, but be patient. In due course, you will be able
to concentrate your attention at the eye centre. Enter within
and give up all thoughts of the external world. You will
achieve everything.

First comes the Jyoti—the Celestial Flame—out of which
emanates Divine Melody. Concentrate your attention on It
and, focussing your subtle mind on the vision, penetrate It.
Continue this practice every day, giving up love for the world
and increasing it for Nam. Desire for Nam grows only by

virtue of constant contact with the Master within. The company of worldly men again pulls us down to the level of the senses. Hence Satsang—Guru's company—is most essential. Our love for the Guru enables us to give up the path of the mind and turn within.

When the seeker follows the instructions of the Guru, beholds the vision of the Celestial Flame, listens to the Divine Music and merges himself in the Word, he goes beyond the sphere of mind and matter. Then by constant practice of Nam, he gets true liberation and ascends to the abode of the Supreme Father.

This is not a small attainment. Whatever may be the trials and tribulations, put up with them willingly, for it is a sure sign that the soul is on its way up. You have found the Path to the Region of Immortality, the Land of Truth, and placed your feet on the ladder of Nam. Climb up and come to the Realm of the Master. On the way, you will cross the Region of Sunn (Void), the Region of Maha Sunn (Great Void), then the Region of 'I-less-ness,' where the soul recognizes its identity with Nam, and ultimately merges in Sat Nam—the Lord Supreme—by faithfully following the directions of the Master. This, however, happens only when the Supreme Lord, in His great mercy, awakens in us love for Himself because of which we begin our search and meet an Adept who is in touch with Him, get the secret of Nam and carry out daily the prescribed course (exercises) under His inspiring guidance. Once we get attached to Nam, we have nothing to worry about, for He watches over us as does a mother over her infant babe. Such opportunities do not come every day. Fortunate, indeed, are we to be incarnated in a human body. We should, therefore, get in touch with someone acquainted with Nam and, on learning the technique from Him, contact Nam.

When the Lord, in His mercy and grace, wants to take us

unto Himself, He does so by imparting the secret of Nam, the Word, through a Master. We develop spiritually in the lap of the Master within, and the Word protects us.

> Make thou friend with 'gurumukh'
> And be devoted to 'Satguru.'
> Thus cut asunder the chain of birth and death;
> Then shalt thou attain eternal bliss.

> --*Adi Granth*

To recapitulate:

1. Soul, essence of the Supreme Being, has lost its way to its true Home.

2. During its descent from the purely Spiritual Realm to the physical one, it got three coverings, the causal, astral and physical bodies, and completely forgot its Royal origin.

3. In association with the mind and the senses, it chained itself firmly to the wheel of birth and death and thus suffered untold misery and privations in different lives and species.

4. It did not avail itself of the human form given by the Creator to effect its release. It was dissipated in sensuous pursuits.

5. The merciful Lord, seeing its miserable plight, came into Master's garb to awaken it from deep slumber.

6. The need is to come in contact with such a Master, learn the technique from Him, carry out spiritual practices with ceaseless persistence and unshakable faith, and thus return Home and merge into the occean of which the soul is a drop.

7. This, however, happens only when He so wills it.

6

In the universe is utter darkness

If one were to withdraw his mind from sensual pleasures and were to attach himself to the Sound Current, he would go back to Sach Khand. Then there would be no more coming and going. All this is within one's self, and whoever 'goes in' according to the instructions of a Master reaches his Home.

Seeing the world in its true light, Soami Ji observes that there is nothing but utter darkness and misery in this world. It is indeed a place where the blind are leading the blind. The slogan 'eat, drink and be merry' is altogether confusing and in reality no one is happy in this wide world. A visit to the hospitals will show the amount of distress and suffering there and how people die in agony. In the cemeteries or the cremation grounds, look how the bereaved ones undergo anguish! The seemingly rich have a heavy load of cares and worries heaped on them and this breaks them completely. "Uneasy lies the head that wears the crown." The poor have practically nothing to fall back upon to go through the voyage of life without bitter privations.

The deadly five enemies of human beings, *viz.* lust, anger, avarice, attachment, pride or egotism permit us no rest or peace. Lust pulls us down to the animal plane. Those given to sensual pleasures severely undermine their health and repent their follies ever afterwards. Anger burns up all that is noble. It tears down and annihilates every fine quality of mind and soul. It is a consuming fire born of the fires of destruction. Avarice binds us to material things and clouds our vision of all higher values. It ties us to baser things of earth. Piety, love and kindness gradually disappear. The greedy person has no end to his wants and desires and nothing can ever satiate him. He constantly runs after a mirage. "The poorest man in the world is he who has nothing but money." Attachment or infatuation is the most insidious and deceitful of the passions. One under its sway merely exists in the flesh and renders himself homeless. "Naked and empty-handed one comes here and likewise one departs." Pride or egotism is a malignant kind of selfishness and is the most sturdy and masterful of the baneful five. It has also the greatest longevity. It is the last to surrender. Its fundamental assumption is its own infallibility. Thus lust degrades and disgraces; anger consumes and desroys; greed hardens and petrifies; attachment seduces and binds; and egotism distorts and deceives.

In the sea, fish live upon one another. Likewise on land, one animal lives upon another and so also do the birds. Hawks prey upon sparrows and the small birds devour insects and worms. Tigers and wolves eat goats and sheep, which in turn feed upon plant life. Man, of course, eats everything. In a sphere where one creature eats another, there can hardly be any peace or tranquillity. However one may argue, the fact remains that every being feels pain. Even a worm tries to save its life. The story of Sadna illlustrates this point.

Sadna was a king's butcher. Once, late in the night, the king asked for some fries. As there was no ready meat available, Sadna was ordered to provide some immediately. As he did not like to kill the whole goat for fear that the rest of the meat would spoil in the warm night, he planned merely to castrate a goat for the time being and kill it the next morning for a fresh supply of meat for sale. As he approached the goat with a knife in his hand, the latter spoke thus, to his utter amazement, "Many a time hast thou killed me and so have I done unto thee, O Sadna, but thou art now embarking upon something new."

This incident completely startled the butcher, made him think deeply and was responsible for altering the whole course of his life. He soon gave up his occupation, sought a Mystic Adept and under his guidance attained high spiritual realms. Ever since then he is referred to as Sadna, the Butcher Saint.

The vegetables have one active tattwa (element) which is water; the insects* have two *viz.* air and fire; the birds have three *viz.* water, air and fire; in the higher animals there are four of them *viz.* earth, water, air and fire; while in man all five elements *viz.* earth, air, water, fire and ether are active. The larger the number of active elements a living entity has, the higher it is in the scale of evolution, and naturally the greater is the onus involved in killing it. Or, in other words, the karmic load that one has to carry on killing is in direct proportion to the active elements present in a living being. Therefore, Saints enjoin a completely vegetarian diet on their followers. Besides, food of animal origin drags one down to the animal plane and bars spiritual progress.

Soami Ji likens the whole world to a labyrinth where different species come and go without finding an exit or escape from the wheel of birth and death. The soul is an essence of the Supreme Lord and belongs to Sat Lok. In its descent to the physical world, it has completely forgotten its

---

* There are two types of insects, those which fly, having air and fire as the two active elements in them; and the ones that crawl, as the ant, whose active elements are earth and fire.

true origin and is wholly dominated by mind and senses. Under their sway it performs actions, good and bad, and then repeatedly returns to reap their rewards, "As ye sow, so shall ye reap", and thus goes on the never-ending cycle. "Not one life but many lives hast thou had to pass as animals and insects". At the end of each life, appear the angels of death who deal the soul an appropriate reward or punishment.

The human form is the only privileged one to realize the Supreme Being and one gets it again after countless ages spent in other forms. Yet, even here, the mind and senses overpower the soul.

All the Saints and Sages preach the Truth, bring home to us the transitoriness of every thing in this world, give us the means to effect our release and enable us to join the Eternal Lord. How unfortunate that instead of following them, we abuse and persecute Them! Guru Nanak was told that he had lost his senses and that he should not misguide people. Kabir was treated no better. Christ was crucified. Mansur was stoned to death, Shamas-i-Tabriz was flayed alive, Guru Gobind Singh's two innocent little sons were bricked alive and He himself was persecuted. Gurus Arjan Dev and Tegh Bahadur were subjected to inhuman tortures and they died at the cruel hands of their persecutors. And yet, all this was done in the name of religion at the dictates of our bigoted guides.

Maharaj Sawan Singh Ji used to illustrate the pitiable state of man by relating the following story :-

A bald-headed person who was both blind and deaf, happened to stray into an inn. He exhorted people to take him out but nobody would help. Thereupon he himself began to grope his way, thinking that he would reach and go out of the main gate. When, however, he actually neared the only exit, in response to an itching sensation on his head, he lifted his hand and scratched, and thus passed the exit in the meantime.

Every time he neared the gate the same thing happened and he thus remained in this maze for ever. We mortals behave exactly in the same fashion, every time we get the gift of a human form, instead of utilizing it for God-realization, we turn to sensual pleasures and once again go down into the labyrinth.

The Saints exhort man to rise above the nine portals of the body and urge him to concentrate his attention at the eye centre. There he can contact the Sound, with the help of which he can go up. Guru Amar Das also says the same thing: "Close the nine doors, still the wayward mind and go to the tenth door. There the Anaahat Shabd resounds incessantly, day and night." Now, one may ask, why do we not hear it? Guru Sahib says that one can hear it only with the help of a perfect Master. It is the Shabd which liberates us, which supports all creation, all regions and continents, and the sun, moon and stars. The Master directs us to withdraw our attention and to concentrate it at the eye centre, where we can contact and eventually merge in the Sound Current. But, without a Perfect Master, even when we think we are turning to Spiritual Practices, we follow paths which are blind alleys. Neither renunciation, nor penances, nor learning, nor pilgrimages can ever bring True Bliss. These practices are like churning water, which can bring out nothing. Going within and contacting Nam, is like churning milk and producing butter.

Soami Ji says that the worldly man is indeed unfortunate, for all his attention is centered in the world. How can a Master take him up, a bundle of filth that he is? To Shabd he is not united. Every thought of the world and the worldly pleasures immediately pulls him down, away from the eye centre. All the same, the washerman must do his duty. He must scrub and clean the dirty clothes. The Master is the washerman for the soul.

The more one devotes himself to Shabd, the more he is purified. But if he takes to counting beads or performing austerities, little do they help him. It only develops egotism.

Nam is not to be found in books. Even if we read all holy scriptures but do not follow the path of Surat Shabd, we are like the 'chandool' bird which parrot-like, imitates all sounds.

Soami Ji tells us that if we want to tread the Spiritual Path, we must learn the technique from an Adept, then go within and unite with the Shabd or the Sound Current. Gradually, our extremities begin to get benumbed, till we actually lose all sensation and behold radiant light within. 'It is now time,' says Soami Ji, "that you should begin to get yourself detached from the world and practise the method of Surat Shabd, for there is no other way." Guru Amar Das also says the same thing: "Without Shabd all is darkness inside; neither do you secure your objective nor do you cease your coming and going."

To recapitulate:

1. This world is full of gloom and misery. None here is happy.

2. The only escape lies in the human body.

3. Recitals, penances and pilgrimages are utterly futile and may be likened to churning water.

4. It is only with the grace of a living Satguru that we can close the nine doors, still the mind, enter the Tenth one and contact Nam which constantly resounds there.

5. This is the only way. No other exists.

7

Axioms of Spirituality

'AXIOM' is a self-evident truth, requiring no demonstrations; a universally accepted principle. We shall now talk about axioms of Sant Mat (the teachings of the Saints)

1. Nobody is happy in this world

Some complain of unemployment and poverty, others of disease, death in the family or some other distress. Everywhere a tide of pain, misery, grief and suffering seems to engulf makind.

> Nanak! all the world is steeped in pain,
> Happy are those, whom doth Nam sustain.

Muslim philosophers have named this world, 'The Home of Distress.'

The world is divided into two parts, water and land. In water, big fish live upon the small ones, and are themselves eaten up by still bigger ones. On the land, big birds eat the small ones and the latter make worms and flies their food. Lions and tigers make smaller animals their prey, and thus it goes on. Man kills all. Nothing is safe from him.

And yet life is very dear to everyone. Imagine the agony of dumb creatures that are daily butchered to provide us food, and the distress of those that are wounded or killed when we are out hunting. The human form, that was granted to us for the sublime purpose of God-realization, is spent in tyranny towards His beings. When man sinks so low, he is worse than a beast. The beast kills only to satisfy its hunger, but man does it for pleasure, notwithstanding the fact that the slightest injury to his own person sends him reeling with pain and he demands immediate relief. What a strange world to live in, which has no security nor peace! No one knows when death will overtake or what catastrophe will befall one.

2. This world is not our True Home

We are in an alien land where nothing is either permanent or our own. All around us is matter and mind made up of the five elements: earth, water, fire, air and akash (the matter that surrounds the earth beyond the air and, for want of a better word, is called ether). Soul, on the other hand, is a denizen of Sach Khand, an essence of the Ocean of Light and Bliss, pure, radiant and transcendent. It is a drop of the ocean of eternal happiness but, in its association with mind, for many ages, has gathered so much dross that it has completely forgotten its origin and has come to believe that this world is its real abode. Soul is tied down with mind, which in its turn is led by the five senses. It thus suffers the consequences of this unfortunate association and has to go through the long chain of life and death. It is in the human form alone that it may come in contact with a perfect Adept, get the secret of Nam from Him and by devotedly practising it, attain liberation.

> Like grass have I grown many times;
> Seven hundred and seventy forms have I been.

--Rumi

Guru Arjan Dev says:

> Many times have you been born as worms
> and flies;
> Many times have you been born as deer,
> sheep and swine;
> Many times have you been born as birds,
> horses and trees;
> After numerous ages have you received
> this human body;
> Therefore, meet the Lord now.
> This is the only time.

3. It is only in the human form that the Soul can realize God and retrace its footsteps Homeward

None other of the eight million and four hundred thousand species has this capacity. Man alone has this privilege. Even gods and angels pine for it. The human body is the exit through which one can get out of the vast prison and thereby put an end to all pain and misery.

But alas! we do not give up the pleasures of the senses. Our mind has become so feeble and erring that it finds itself unable to withstand the ravishing sense pleasures and falls an easy prey to temptation. It is, however, never satiated. The more it gets, the more it desires. It perfectly realizes that the reaction of all 'bhogas' (sense enjoyments) is pain, sorrow and dejection, yet it persists in its silly pursuits. Beware! no action in this world goes without bearing fruit. Every action has its reaction. The worst reaction is that of lust.

Guru Arjan Dev says:

> For one moment of lust enjoyment,
> Ten million days of agony await thee.

This adds up to thirty-three thousand years of agony for one moment of sensual pleasure. Only a fool would enter into such a bad bargain. What fools are we! If the result of pleasure is pain, how can it be pleasure? A wise man always keeps the ultimate result in mind.

> Blessed is the person
> Who always keeps his eye on the goal.
>
> --*Maulana Rum*

But what is the remedy? How to dissuade the rabid mind from following this insane course, which takes it to destruction? In order to find a suitable remedy we must consider the nature of the mind. We know that it is fond of pleasure but it never sticks to one thing. It constantly keeps flitting from one to another. Nothing can keep it engaged for long. As soon as it sees something better, sweeter or prettier than what it has, it runs after that and throws away what it has in hand. The mind is never constant. The same is true of its love and attachment. It will readily give up all if we provide it with something sweeter and more absorbing than the worldly pleasures. That 'something' is within us, in our own body. It is resounding above and behind our eyes in the form of sweet Music, which the Saints call Shabd, Bani, Nam, Word, Anhad Shabd, Sound Current or Audible Life Stream. When the mind hears this Celestial Music, all worldly pleasures become tasteless.

All the Saints and Sages say that God is within us and that all our sorrows and worries will come to an end, only when we turn our attention inward.

Christ says:

The Kingdom of God is within you.

Guru Nanak, Kabir, Tulsi Das, Soami Ji, Prophet Mohammed,

all say the same thing. But we search for Him without, in temples, mosques, and churches; in rites and rituals; in scriptures and holy books; in penances and charities. All these, undoubtedly, have some merit in them but they keep us confined to lower worlds and cannot take us beyond the sphere of action and reaction. For reaping the reward of good deeds, we have to be born again in this phenomenal world. We can get true liberation only by totally withdrawing our attention from the outside and concentrating it at the eye centre as instructed by the Master.

4. God-realization is not possible without a perfect Master

He alone can show us how to vacate the nine portals of the body and enter the tenth which leads to our Eternal Home. The Vedas, Smrities, other holy scriptures and the Saints and Sages of all religions stress the need for a Mystic Adept for transport into subtle realms. Actually, man needs a teacher at every step from the time of his birth. He has learnt nothing without one. His first guru is his mother who teaches him how to sit, stand, walk, eat, drink and dress. Later his father, brothers and sisters take on the onerous role and he begins to prattle. When he grows a little older, his friends and playmates become his guru. Next he goes to schools and colleges where there are any number of them to teach him. Yet when it comes to learning the science of the soul—the most intricate of sciences, rarely do we search for a guru, and without one it is impossible to proceed even an inch on this path. Maulana Rum says:

Even in the streets through which,
You have passed a number of times,
You often miss the way,
If you do not have a guide.
Beware of the way,
Which you have never traversed.
Never go there alone,
Always take a guide.

Not only is it impossible to know God without the help of a Mystic Adept, but without his protecting hand over one, it may be hazardous to make an attempt at going into subtle regions. In this path, many are the temptations to lead us astray, many the pitfalls to drag us down. Without a guide, we are sure to lose the way and fall into the quagmire of delusion and danger. The Perfect Master will show us how and where to enter the body, "the temple of the living God". There are nine outlets which lead to the sense world but the tenth opens into the spiritual regions. This is called the 'Sushmana' gate and is located in the centre behind the eyes. It is through this aperture that we pass beyond matter and mind to reach the Everlasting and Immortal Region where the Supreme Lord–The Creator of all–resides. Austerities and the yoga of Pranayam (breathing) do not take us beyond the six centres. Only the Surat Shabd Yoga, the Yoga of the Audible Life Stream, the Anaahat Shabd of the Upanishads, the Word or Logos of the Bible, can take us to the Highest Region, which is Eternal. This yoga can be taught only by the Saints. Nanak, Kabir, Dadu, Paltu, Maulana Rum, Shams-i-Tabriz, all preached and followed this way.

The Surat Shabd Yoga is not a new science. It has existed ever since the world was made. Saints do not come to establish a new religion, nor a new creed, nor even a new sect. Their mission is simply to liberate the qualified souls from this land of misery, and to guide them back to their Home of Eternal Bliss and Peace. The Saints say:

> Brothers, this world is not your True Home. Nobody is happy here. This is the home of pain and sorrow. Leave this prison-house of evolution and devolution, and return to your own Home. This can be accomplished only while you are in the human body. Take full advantage of this opportunity. Seek a Perfect Master. Learn from Him the Science of Surat Shabd Yoga. Attach yourself to the Voice of God which calls within you at the eye centre. Follow this Divine Melody. Like a Powerful magnet, it will pull you up and take you to the feet of the Lord, whence these Currents emanate.

These are the teachings of the Saints (Sant Mat) in a nutshell. The Saints do not ask you to give up one religion and join another, nor do they ask you to renounce the world or your family, or to change your mode of living. They advise you to live with your wife and children as usual, to carry on your profession and to perform all other duties. They only enjoin you to give some time daily, punctually and regularly to the most important of your duties, which is devotion to God and listening to His voice, the Celestial Sound within.

You are to live in the world, but in a sensible way. Enjoy the world and its objects, but realize their true worth. They are meant to serve you. Take full service from them but do not yourself become their slave. Let not your mind be so entangled in attachment to these objects that, instead of being of service to you, they become your master. Live in the world in the most unconcerned way. Neither should the gift of a kingdom elate you, nor the loss of possessions depress you. Live in the world, but be of God and not of the world. Without actually renouncing, live like one who has renounced it. This is the real 'Sanyas' (renunciation of the world) and has nothing to do with donning a saffron coloured robe or other religious garb. How aptly a Hindu Mystic has portrayed it in the following lines :-

> Even when you have renounced the world,
> And live not in a village or town,
> Nor possess property or chattel of any kind,
> But instead roam about in forests and hills,
> And drink water from brooks and springs,
> Eat whatever is available in the forest,
> Put on no clothes,
> Read scriptures day and night
> And do repetition of 'Om',
> Yet if there is an iota of desire,
> Of worldly pleasure in your mind,
> You are still a householder,
>   through and through.

Both renunciation and attachment pertain to the mind. Outward forms and symbols have nothing to do with them. Enter this garden of the world. Take a walk in it. Enjoy the fragrance of the flowers. Eat fruits and behold the beauties of Nature, but do not get entangled in thorns and prickly shrubs, lest you may get abrasions and wounds.

Earn wealth honestly and spend it well. It is meant for you. Attend to your work during the day. Day is for work. But at night give some time to devotion and contemplation. This is 'your real work'. Just think for a moment. Of all that you do during the day, nothing of it is for yourself. Much that you do is for your family and friends. Daily you spend some time in adorning your body, but realize that even this is not yours and will not accompany you on your last journey. It will stay behind to be buried or cremated.

Your own work is that of doing Simran and Bhajan (the Spiritual Exercises) which will, in due course, liberate you from this vast prison in which you have been confined for countless ages. Life is short. Time is fleeting. Take full advantage of it, and if you have not done 'your own work' already, start doing it now. Seek a True Master and under His guidance attach your soul to the 'Word' and reach your True Home.

PART II

Excerpts from Discourses

Excerpts from Discourses

1. Saints point out that all human beings come into this world for the purpose of realizing the priceless wealth of Nam, but only a few Gurmukhs (devoted souls) succeed in doing so. The rest have to be born again and go through rigorous penance in the mother's womb where they hang head down for nine months under utterly appalling conditions. What sustains the soul during this period is its constant attention in the eye centre and endless entreaties to its Maker to deliver it from this inferno. He constantly prays that in the new life he will ever remember his Creator. However, as soon as he is born, the entire family is jubilant and fondles him. All around him are strange scenes and novel objects. Beholding them, he completely forgets all promises that he assiduously made while in the mother's womb and becomes completely oblivious of his Creator. Ultimately, nothing will remain with him and yet he heeds not the Reality. When he attains youth, he is entirely under the sway of wealth, possessions and sensual enjoyment. God's Name, which was to release him from bondage and suffering, he has completely ignored. He constantly runs after illusion, remains restless and gets weary. Thus he wastes his precious life in baseless pursuits. Neither does he contact the Sound Current nor does he bring his mind under control and consequently remains oblivious of the high purpose for which he was given the human form.

When he reaches old age, reapers in the shape of angles of death come to harvest the field. No one knows where they come from and where do they take him. Only a moment before he claimed everything as his own and Lo ! nothing now belongs to him. He is a total stranger in an unknown land. His wife, children and other relatives and friends, doubtless bewail and bemoan their loss but they cannot retain him and hasten to consign his remains to earth or fire. He goes to a place to which he is entitled in accordance with his deeds and desires. Thus did he pass his old age too without attaining or even starting on the Path of God-realization.

* * *

2. The Saints and Sages laboured hard, attained spiritual heights, discovered certain truths and recorded them in books for our guidance. These are :

First, there is a Maker of this universe. It did not just come about by itself.

Second, the Maker Himself is unchangeable but the world which He has created is constantly undergoing change. Living beings come into this world and then die. The vegetable and the mineral kingdoms are also subject to change. The Creator alone is Eternal and Everlasting. "In the beginning was the Truth (Shabd), at the commencement of the aeons was the Truth, now is the Truth and, O Nanak, ever shall remain the Truth." The word Truth, in this case, implies that which always exists in the same condition without change. It does not connote merely speaking the truth. Whatever exists constantly in the same form, that is the Truth. Only 'He' exists eternally without change.

Third, man alone has the capacity and the privilege to realize God. That is why the Muslims have called man the 'noblest of all creation'. The Hindus have called the human body, 'the Form Divine'. Christ has referred to it as "The temple of the Living God", the Holy Granth Sahib states that out of the eighty-four lac species of living beings man is at the top. Man's uniqueness lies in his ability to realize God within himself. Neither gods nor angels can do so and have necessarily to be born in a human form to reach Him. It, therefore, behoves us to utilize this opportunity for God-realization.

Often it is asked, who are angels? Sages say that souls in human form performed good deeds and, in reward thereof, were given heavens and paradises to live in. However, as soon as the merit of the good deeds is over, such souls are again given birth in this world and they take forms in accordance with their karmas.

Fourth, whenever man realizes God, he realizes Him within himself. He cannot be realized in mountains, forests, idols and places of pilgrimage, nor in scriptures and holy books. Whoever has perceived Him and will perceive Him has done so or will do so only within himself. It is only after realizing Him within, that one begins to see Him everywhere.

Guru Amar Das says:

"Within this house is everything and nothing is without. In the body resideth He Himself, the Transcendent Being, but the ignorant creature given to egoism seeketh Him without."

Lastly, even within himself, man will realize God only when he has reached the third eye. This is accomplished by first withdrawing all the consciousness from the body, up to the eye centre, and then taking it up by means of Shabd or Nam. Nam itself can be obtained only from an Adept, and one will come across such an Adept only through the Grace of God. To sum up : There is no salvation without Nam, no Nam without a Master, and neither is possible without the Grace of God. So, first comes the Grace of God, second, that of the Sat Guru, third, the initiation into Nam and last but not the least, the effort of the disciple.

* * *

3. In this world of doubt and delusion, of darkness, pain and grief, nobody ever knows the result of his actions;

nor does he know his beginning or end. Wearily does he go down the scale of creation and finds peace nowhere. Soami Ji says that Masters alone reveal the secret of the inaccessible Lord and it is through realizing Him that the soul gets rid of mind and matter and the untold misery caused by them. Intense yearning for the Lord is the primary prerequisite, for it is this that purifies and strengthens the mind so that it begins to appreciate the futility of religious observances and rituals. Through His immense Grace does one escape the cycle of birth and death. By completely withdrawing one's attention to the eye centre and stopping all the nine outlets does one gain complete control over one's mind and senses. No longer does one depend on merely reading scriptures and holy books, but attains perfect Bliss by traversing the Path within.

He throws to the winds the worldly name and fame and likewise all rites and rituals. At the altar of devotion to Nam, does he obtain real knowledge. Priceless is Nam, but only real Saints know its true worth. The Limitless, the Everlasting or the Unfathomable is realized beyond the three worlds, only when the soul contacts Shabd or Nam. This technique, which converts vile sinners into Saints, is known as Surat Shabd Yoga. Overflowing love for the Master and complete surrender to Him are the essentials for success.

* * *

4. Only in the human form can one realize God, and it is only within, that He can be realized. This, in turn, is only possible with the help of a Perfect Adept. The main obstruction to God-realization is our own mind. It is fond of pleasures and, in running after them during countless ages, it has become extermely fickle.

No one pleasure of this world can keep it satisfied or tied down for long. As a child one's pleasures find expressions in love for parents, later in that of friends and playmates, and when he reaches adolescence, in love for wife and children. As he grows older, he strives for wealth, property, power and prestige. He continues to seek one pleasure after another, thus truly chasing a mirage.

The soul is dominated by the mind and the latter in its turn is ruled by the senses. Thus, wherever the mind goes, the soul perforce has to go with it. If the mind were to cease running after the things of this world and become motionless, the soul would immediately fly to its True Home—Sat Lok. It is the mind that has tied human beings to this world and, through its good and bad actions, keeps them treading the eternal wheel to reap their consequences. Thus the Satsang and discourses on Nam and Satguru are specifically directed to the mind. On listening to them it may turn away from sensual pleasures and find refuge at the eye centre, from where its upward journey begins. Then the Nam which is constantly reverberating above this centre pulls up both mind and soul. Hearing this Celestial Melody, the mind spontaneously exclaims : "Here is the bliss that I have been hankering after all this time !" It now needs nothing else, and all the worldly pleasures turn insipid and tasteless. Thus the only way to control the mind and end its misery is to attach it to Nam. Nam alone can restrain and satisfy the mind. All other practices are utterly futile, for even when apparently successful they not infrequently let a person down badly. These practices are like confining a snake in a basket. So long as it remains closed under a tight lid, the snake may be harmless, but the fear of its making an escape is ever there. Whenever the snake gets an opportunity, it will not fail to bite. Nam is beyond the sphere of mind. Only when the Master is realized within, will His Omniscience become clear for ever.

* * *

5. God can be realized by human beings alone. It is their exclusive privilege. No other creature has this gift. Even by man, this can be done only by concentrating one's attention at the third eye focus and listening to the Sound that reverberates there day and night. This sound is called Nam, Word or Shabd. Everybody lives within the confines of the nine apertures, *viz.*, two eyes, two ears, two nostrils, the mouth and the two lower outlets. These 'doors' of the body establish connection of the mind and soul with the outer world while the tenth 'gate' that lies hidden at the eye centre connects the soul with God. So long as the mind dwells in the nine apertures, it remains in the domain of illusion, which is made up of three gunas. The latter are robbers that steal all our treasure and make us completely forget our true self. The three gunas are Sattva, Rajas and Tamas. Tamas leads completely to negative action and destruction. Rajas binds one to the worlds through various snares and allurements, and keep him ever restless. Sattva, on the other hand, produces virtues like compassion, righteousness and devotion. The human form is like the top rung of the ladder. Next to it is the roof. None can realize God, unless he transcends the three gunas. Beyond them lies the 'Sehaj' state which begins in Par Brahm and ends in Sat Lok. This is a state of utmost tranquillity and everlasting bliss. 'Sehaj' cannot be attained in the three 'gunas', for the three 'gunas' are in delusion. It is only met within the fourth realm and is found by the devotees of a guru. Guru Sahib explains thus :

> He who attains 'Sehaj' attains God.
> Neither doth he die, nor tread the eternal wheel.

When a person reaches this Realm, he ends the cycle of birth and death and becomes the chosen of God. He who sent you calls you back; come Home with the bliss of 'Sehaj'.

The way to attain this stage is by constant devotion to Nam, as revealed by a True Master, and complete surrender to His will. "We are not to question why; ours is but to do and die." Our own horizon of vision is limited, while that of the Master is boundless. The so-called intellect and reasoning are powerless. The Master's commands are for the disciples' lasting good.

* * *

6. In their spiritual research, all the Sages and Saints have come to the same conclusion; namely :

(*a*) There is one God.

(*b*) He can be realized by human beings alone, and the essential prerequisites are a life of piety, contentment, chastity and forgiveness.

(*c*) Human beings can find Him only within and not outside.

(*d*) The way to find Him is to contact Shabd by completely concentrating the attention at the eye centre and making the mind motionless.

(*e*) This, however, happens only when God wills the soul to return to its True Home. Shabd realization in the company of mystics is the highest of all actions; but, "Only he attains it, O Nanak, who hath it already imprinted in his destiny."

(*f*) Then, a person seeks a Perfect Adept, learns from Him the technique of retiring within and, by His grace and guidance attains the Nam that merges him with the Lord. "How discerning is our Lord; Himself as saint is He known." "Without Satguru one cannot have devotion, nor attachment to Nam." Guru Nanak repeatedly exhorts us to restrain our mind from wandering out, to keep it still, to prevent it from yearning for anything but the Lord, and then to listen to the immanent Nam. If we do not adopt this course, we inevitably fall into the hands of angels of death and nothing but utter misery and pain engulf us. Nothing avails one save devotion to Nam, which is the only Reality. It, therefore, behoves us all to cease running outside and to remain merged in the Sound Current all the time. For in this way alone shall we obtain permanent release from continuous bondage.

The true Adept is in essence God Himself. Outwardly he has human form, but inwardly he is Lord Divine.

> God and His mystics are one,
> Just as the wave riseth from the ocean
> And mergeth into it again,
> So doth he descend from God
> And unto Him he returneth.
> In this have thou no doubt.
>
> *--Granth Sahib*

He lives in the world, but is not of the world. He is completely absorbed in the Shabd. His soul is united with God. He is an ocean of mercy. He is the greatest benefactor of all. The gift of Nam He bestows on people and takes them out of the realm of duality and relativity.

> He has turned man into a divine being
> And no time has he taken to do so.
>
> *--Granth Sahib*

He comes into this world to unite us with God. He is above desire and want, and likewise transmutes us. Whoever comes in contact with such a true Master and devotedly follows His directions, beholds the ultimate Reality and becomes one with it.

> In the company of the Mystics
> Is found the true philosopher's stone

That turneth base metals (sinners)
Into pure gold (Saints).

--Maulana Rum

* * *

7. Saints throughout the ages have proclaimed that God is ever bountiful and there is no limit to His grace. While man may get weary of asking, He is never tired of giving. His treasures are unlimited and there is nothing a man desires that he cannot get. Yet in the whole world there is none who has all his desires fulfilled. This apparent contradiction is due to the fact that we cannot see the whole show at one glance. We see only isolated acts and unrelated episodes, which can be easily reconciled by realizing that the soul is indestructible and, in the phenomenon of death, it merely changes its garment and transfers its field of action. But its accounts go with it wherever it is reborn and it is in its new life that the soul consummates its unrealized desires and gets entangled in new ones. It is, however, not necessary that this may only happen in the human form.

It is the desires that create Karmas, and the Karmas lead to rounds of birth and death. Saints, therefore, exhort us to cut at their very root and to ask for nothing save the Lord Himself, for when one owns the very source of the bounty, there is no dearth of His gifts.

Vain are the pleasures and pursuits of this world, for they lead to endless misery and suffering. The only escape from their clutches and from utter ignorance that so thickly pervades the scene, is contact with Nam, which alone can afford lasting relief and liberation. "Nam is true nectar, but how can we describe it? He alone that drinketh it, knoweth it."

* * *

8.   The necessary preparation for 'Arti'* is :

(*a*)   Work hard on the path shown by the Master. When
the mind finds little apparent progress despite its
labour, it grows restless and begins to feel pangs of
separations from the Master. This develops into an
intense longing and ardent love for Him, which
actually burns up all worldly desires, frees the soul
from its shackles and makes it fit for mystic transport.
This fervent love is the essence of all spiritual
discipline and it is attained by faithfully carrying
out the devout practices as explained by the Master
at the time of Initiation.

(*b*)   The impediments in the way of spiritual progress
are the worldly attachments and allurements. The
soul is bound tight with the fetters of lust and greed,
and continually runs after one illusion or another.
Soami Ji has enumerated the different kinds of chains
that tie the soul to this world, prevent it from
concentration at the Master's Feet and from rising
above its earthly abode. The first chain is that of
body itself, the second of wife, the third of sons, the
fourth of grandsons, the fifth of great grandsons, the
sixth of wealth and possessions, the seventh of vanity
and self-righteousness and the eighth of social
customs, rites, rituals and the like. They all lead the
soul astray, debase it and make it completely forgetful
of the Creator. These strong chains can be cut asunder
only by devotedly following the course outlined by
a Perfect Adept. There is and can be no other way of
escape.

---

*   'Arti' connotes the true worship of the Shabd within. Outwardly it is a ritual for
worship with lights.

(c) Soami Ji further says : "The Master bestowed upon me the secret of Shabd. By concentrating my attention at the eye centre I came into contact with the Sound Current. There I beheld the Radiant form of my Master. Only then did I become a true disciple and a deserving one, and went beyond matter and mind." The reason for this is not far to seek. The astral form of the Master is so brilliant and magnetic that the soul cannot but shed its gross matter and ultimately merge in the Ocean of which it is a drop.

* * *

9. After creating human beings and others in the universe, Brahm attached to each soul his agent in the shape of mind, to confine the soul to his domain. The specific commands to the mind are, "Never let the soul go near Shabd nor reveal to it the secret thereof."

When the hour of destiny strikes, everyone must leave this theatre of action and his earthly remains are buried or cremated. Every soul must essentially close its eyes upon the scene of action and take a new birth called for by its karmas. The law of karma is universal. It is the fixed and the immutable law of nature. Each soul must reap what it has sown. Every soul shall have to bear the exact consequences of its actions.

Matter and Mind so wholly engross the individual attention that one remains ignorant of the 'Royal Road' leading to Sat Lok, the 'pure spiritual region'. "Without Shabd the soul is blind; so where can it go ? The way to Shabd it findeth not but falleth into delusion again and again."

Victory over the Negative Power and the complete surrender of the mind can be achieved only by contacting Nam with the help of a True Master. "Hearing the celestial melody, he breaketh the fetters of illusion and attaineth Eternal Bliss."

* * *

10. The soul cannot ascend until the 'Nirat' or the power of seeing is developed within. The two faculties – one of hearing and the other of seeing – are utilized by the soul for its mystic transport. Some disciples devote their attention to hearing the sound, but do not try to fix their 'Nirat' inside. This is a mistake, for unless the attention is fixed at the eye centre, the mind does not become motionless, and there is little pleasure in the practice.

When the 'Nirat' or the inner vision is fully developed, the sound that emanates from within, becomes increasingly distinct. The soul, however, must catch the finest note; by means of which it will ascend to higher regions. When it reaches 'Daswan Dwar', an important stage in his spiritual path, it will go beyond the meshes of illusion and the negative power.

* * *

11. All Saints stress the need of loving devotion to the Master for spiritual advancement. It is this devotion that enables us to contact Nam and listen to the sweet Melody resounding within at the eye centre. This alone is Guru Mat (teachings of the Saints). All else is deception and illusion, for within the confines of mind and matter we utterly follow Man Mat (dictates of mind and senses). Bhakti Marg (path of love and devotion) is the Royal Road leading to our Eternal Home, and once we commence our journey on it, no matter where we go or the stage we reach, the protecting and guiding hand of the Satguru is ever there to escort us onwards. There can be no matter of doubt in our finally reaching the true destination, if we have complete faith in Him. Hollow are all other methods. They are like empty shells. Hold fast, therefore, to the Bhakti Marg, Give up so-called knowledge, scholarship and wisdom, surrender completely to His Will and remain within the commandments of the Master. Thus one becomes a true Guru

Mukh (a devotee of the Guru). "So long as instructions from a mystic Adept thou dost not get, Him thou canst not find, for too subtle is He for the grip of reason."

Intense longing, ardent love and unfailing devotion denote the same thing. They are the three inseparables in Guru Mat – the path of the Masters, the essential ingredients of true Bhakti. All the rest are innovations of the mind. The Trinity of God, soul and Satguru is indeed one long chain of Infinite Love. The devotee of the Lord also manifests the same love. The individual soul is the drop, the Satguru the stream, and God the vast Ocean. Just as a drop of rain gets polluted with coarse matter during its fall on the earth, so does the soul, in its descent to the physical world, obtain coverings of mind and matter and lose its lustre. Nothing save pure love pervades in Sach Khand, the abode of the Ultimate Reality. Illusion has no place there. It is truly the Fountainhead of pure, unalloyed love, eternal and limitless. None but the Saints have access to it and only the Perfect Adept abides there. Therefore, develop utmost devotion and abiding love for the Satguru.

Once we realize that our Creator is one; that we are the sons of the same Father; that we are drops from the same Ocean of Love, there can be no discord. Peace and Bliss can be the only fruit. The drop of water, on coming in contact with the earth becomes muddy, but on evaporation it regains its purity and joins the clouds. The soul is like this drop. It is corrupted with desires of the mind. When it ascends to higher realms, it is completely shorn of its gross matter and is thus rendered absolutely pure.

Man is verily a mine of the Nectar of Immortality. "In thine own self is the nectar full to the brim; but without Guru thou gettest not its taste; just as the deer knoweth not its musk but keepeth wandering hither and thither in search of it. Without Shabd every man is mad, and wasteth away his life in vain. 'Shabd' is the real nectar; and Guru's devotee alone findeth it O Nanak." It is through loving devotion to the Master that we get the secret of Nam. Even though in the beginning the intensity of love is not pronounced, with constant devotion and scrupulous adherence to the directions given by the Master, this deficiency is soon made up. In due course love wells up as an overflowing stream and liberates the soul forever from the ties of the world.

We are all the recipients of immense Grace. We are born as human beings, who alone have the capacity of God-realization. We have got a True Master who has granted us the boon of Nam and has come to reside permanently within the eye centre of each disciple. It is now clear that our duty is to live up to His injunctions, develop constant love and devotion, and thereby reap the reward of Eternal Bliss.

"In the union of the soul with Shabd is happiness; in the realization of God is Bliss."

* * *

12. Whoever wishes to tread the path of devotion has essentially to fulfill certain conditions. He has to rise above position, prestige and social status; has to turn deaf ears to slander, criticism and ridicule, and has to completely ignore calumny, taunt and censure of society. "Censure and rebuke of the world act as guards in the market of love and devotion. They remove a person's dirt and cleanse him." He has to face resolutely the opposition of his near and dear ones; has to shun rites and rituals that take his attention 'outside', has to give up cunning and deceit as well as lust and greed. "Devotion is impossible for the lustful, the ill-tempered and the covetous." "Truly brave is the person who for this purpose, is ready to give up caste and family."

He has to reach a stage of equanimity where neither honour should elate him nor dishonour or disgrace depress him. "Some praise you, others revile you. Treat both alike with indifference and detachment." He has to be completely fearless and bold, for without His Will nothing can or will happen. Worry can only deflect and debar spiritual progress. Not until he has cast off all dread and apprehension, can he be firm in devotion and sustain it. Those who insult him are totally ignorant of the rare greatness of devotion and the bliss it bestows, and are themselves the losers. He has to turn his back on the world and its pursuits, and tread instead the path of his Master. Once he fortifies himself with Guru's grace and lovingly follows His directions, nothing can upset him.

Practice maketh a man perfect. Even though he starts with misgivings, in due course, perseverance and sincere effort enable him to develop a strong fervour and piety. Mere show can lead him nowhere. An antidote for lack of devotion is more and more steadfast devotion. With unwavering faith in the Master, devotion unfailingly leads to realization of 'Nam' – the Elixir against all suffering in the world. Soami ji lays stress on 'Bhakti'. There is no other way to realize Him and to free the soul forever.

* * *

13. Guru Arjan Sahib presents a vivid picture of the world as he sees it. Both spiritually and physically, almost the whole of mankind is sick at heart and in dire distress. The five passions eat into their vitals incessantly and drive them virtually mad. Not a man escapes from their venom. In addition to a deplorable mental and spiritual plight, physical ills take a heavy toll and make men utterly weary and worn. The young grow to old age in the vain quest for peace. Everywhere there is a constant fever of unrest and never-ending search for what they never find. It is indeed a mirage that eludes them all. Wealth, health, power and so-called pleasures are so short-lived that they pass in a flash and leave people completely confounded. The sensual pursuits leave them on the verge of bankruptcy. The greater the indulgence, the more diseased the bodies and the keener the misery and suffering. An instant of pleasant sensation, a brief delirium of power, a mad moment of passion—all end in intense pain and sorrow, and yet man constantly chases them. He turns his back on 'Nam' which alone can release him from untold privations and lead him to Eternal Bliss.

People have come to believe that this world is permanent and that all its objects are imperishable. This is untrue and is of course the play of illusion. We daily see people departing from our midst. We actually take part in cremating or burying them. Change is writ large on everything everywhere. Pleasures that appear sweet and enchanting are short-lived and end in pain. Our ambitions have no end and are limitless, one giving rise to another and that to yet another. Thus is woven a long chain of desires that bring us to this earthly existence over and over again. Instead of loosening our bonds, we tighten their grip by our own actions, and remain here forever.

The soul, an essence of the Supreme Being, is here dominated by the mind and the latter in turn is led by the senses, with the result that the whole creation is running wild and out of control, under the impulse of one or more of the five passions. Thus the mind goes astray and in its never-ending pursuits, finds little repose or respite. Continually does it come to grief, but it does not seem to heed the lessons of its bitter experiences. Mind is an excellent servant but a very bad master. Rightly used, it may be made to work wonders, but if allowed to assert itself in a lawless manner, it may bring unspeakable disaster. The right course should have been for the soul to control the mind and the mind to guide the senses and thus reverse the grim situation where men have forgotten their high origin the purpose of their sojourn on this planet and their real destination. The more they attach themselves to the things of the world, the farther they move away from their Home. The only remedy lies in seeking a True Adept and following the path of Nam – an absolute 'Must' for ending the rounds of birth and death.

All form, beauty and fascination of the world is nothing but illusion. It is a well-designed net that ensnares us all. The five passions–lust, anger, avarice, attachment and pride – are commissioned by the Negative Power to mislead both mind and soul, and make trouble for them. Impelled by desires, the soul gets caught like a bird that tries to pick inviting grains from a hidden snare. It is verily in hostile land and is surrounded by passions, which are never satisfied. One temptation follows another in quick succession, leaving behind a trail of insipidness. In such circumstances, the soul is helpless. It can only sit back and watch the wreck, and suffer in silence. It can come into its own only when it contacts 'Nam' through the grace of a Master. The world worships the gift and not the Giver. But it is devotion to the latter alone that can liberate us.

There is none in this world who is beyond temptation. It is the Lord's Grace that can save an individual from its operation. The Lord is omnipotent and omniscient, and no one can question His doings. He may, if He so likes, involve us deeply in the charms of this transitory world or make us rise above them and take to the path of the Masters. Who dare advise the Lord, what to do and what not to do ? The 'Harijans' (devotees of the Lord) cross this vast ocean with His help. They concentrate at the eye centre, go 'within' and contact 'Nam', while the pleasure seekers dissipate their energy in the external attractions. The function of Maya is to draw our attention outwards and downwards, and that of 'Nam' inwards and upwards.

* * *

14. When there is drought and fodder is scarce, cowherds move from place to place with their cattle in search of suitable pastures. When they find such places, they merely make temporary arrangements to pass their time in the full knowledge that soon they will return to their own homes. Our sojourn in this world is an equally short and temporary one, and we also need to build only temporary connections. We are not to stay here forever. One day we have to leave family, friends and possessions. Even our own body will remain behind. Little do we know on what day the angels of death will summon us. We must, therefore, not regard the worldly possessions as our own, but as loaned to us for the time being that we may both preserve them and use them profitably. Our life in this planet is like a night and when this is over, we must start afresh on our journey. We must not become so bound up with worldly interests that we have to continually return to it. Its attractions will doubtless bring us back. By desire we are bound to the object of desire. "There have been countless mighty rulers in this world. They used to speak of 'I' and 'mine', but when they died, they took away with them not a single straw." We must, therefore, turn our back on the outside world and retire 'within' to obtain deliverance from its agony and affliction.

Life is like an empty dream. There is nothing real about it. Just as a blossom does not last for long, so does not life. As in a dramatic performance the various actors come to play their part as king, queen, villain, etc., and on its conclusion go their own way, forgetting all about the ephemeral relationships, so is the world a big stage where we come to perform the predestined roles and then depart. Like the dramatic performance, our attachments in life are unreal and only for the purpose of carrying out our allotted jobs. As a guest does not insist on the comforts of a house or its surroundings, apart from what his host can offer, so does it befit us all to live in this world during our temporary sojourn, resigned to His Will and the provisions He has made for us.

The whole creation is engaged in feverish and senseless pursuits. It suffers dismay and disappointment at every step. We shed plenty of tears for money, wife and children, and suffer agony and anguish through loss of them. But if we were to weep earnestly for God for only one day, we would surely attain Him. We pass our lives fruitlessly like a wageless labourer, who works hard the whole day and comes home empty-handed. The real aim of human life remains unattained. Thus we lose both, this world and the next. Futile is human birth without 'Nam' realization. "If a man knoweth not his self during his life time, he cannot even imagine the ills that may be in store for him after death."

It behoves us all to sing the praises of the Lord. The real chanting is not with physical voice but by going 'inside' and contacting the sweet melody. "By recitation He cannot be known; in delusion are all sects; By Guru's Grace is God realized and the tongue tasteth the Nectar of His bliss."

The human form which is our most precious gift and which we have obtained after wandering through the eighty-four lac species is the top of all creation. It is wise to put it to appropriate use and rise above the domain of Kal. "Who knoweth not Nam, he is blind and deaf; for what doth he come into the world ?" There are two ladders; the ladder of 'eighty-four' which leads down and the ladder of 'Nam' that leads up. The one ushers us into darkness and delusion, and the other into light and refulgence. We must jump from the former to the latter and hold it firmly. It is through this ladder that, with devotion and love, we can ascend to higher realms and ultimately return to our Eternal Home.

* * *

15. Repeatedly have the saints stressed the uniqueness of 'Nam'. Without 'Nam' the chain of births and deaths does not cease. 'Nam' can be contacted only with the help of one who is proficient in it and is indeed a True Master.

The physical body performs its functions only so long as the soul resides within it. In fact, everything in existence is entirely dependent upon soul for its life and activity. Form, beauty and colour all owe themselves to its spark. When the soul departs, the earthly remains possess neither value nor purpose. In a fleeting moment, the individual passes beyond mortal ken and becomes altogether a stranger to his near and dear ones. They hasten to consign him to fire or earth.

It is only in the human body that God can be realized. If, therefore, we train ourselves, with the help of a True Adept, to withdraw the currents of mind and soul from the nine apertures of the body and focus them at the eye centre, we can contact 'Nam' which alone can result in perfect peace and bliss, both here and in the higher realms. We are then like an accomplished bride who is honoured for her attainments, both in her own house and that of her parents-in-law. Knowing that this world is full of pain and grief where not even kings are happy, it is only proper that we turn to the region of 'Nam'. "Nam is the antidote for all ills, and all sins doth it wash away."

Death overtakes all. Blessed are those who die daily while living; that is to say, they have learned to vacate the body during their lifetime through Surat Shabd Yoga and to contact the Master 'within'. Such souls are the happiest brides, for they have realized their Lord in this very life and have thus consummated their union. "True Wisdom hath he in whom Nam abideth and who has been united to Nam. Never again is he separated from it and in his True Home doth he find abode."

* * *

16. Do not love the outward forms, for they are not only subject to change but will also perish. Instead, we must seek Him, who alone is permanent and unchangeable. This Supreme

Creator, the Final Cause, One without a second, is Nam, Shabd or 'Sach' (Truth). He is also called the Heavenly Sound. He cannot be comprehended with intellect, for intellect is limited and He is limitless. He is beyond the reach of mind and reasoning, which actually bar spiritual progress by raising senseless doubts and misgivings. The poor and the lowly, who have simplicity and innocence, advance on the Path distinctly faster. No man ever achieved spiritual progress by a process of logic. "Neither by contemplation nor by intellectual discourse, can we realize Him." The only way to do so is to seek a true Master and follow His instructions implicitly. Once we contact Nam, we leave the phenomenal world with its pain and sorrow behind and enter into the world of Bliss. There is no substitute whatever for Nam. All other methods – recitals, penances, pilgrimages – are utterly futile. They keep us confined to the domain of duality and illusion and its eternal wheel. "In Kalyuga, Nam alone doth sustain. Save Nam all else is false and vain."

The sensual world is indifferent to the fate of the soul. Despite the misery it goes through, it still clings firmly to the momentary pleasures. "The camel loves to eat thorny bushes. The more it eats the thorns, the more the blood gushes from its mouth. Still it must eat thorny plants and will not give them up." If we remove the benighted soul from his worldly surroundings to a spiritual environment, it will pine away. The worm that grows in filth feels supremely happy there. It thrives in filth and if we take it out, it either dies or finds its way back there. "Who hath left out Nam, in vain doth he perform other recitals. Like a germ in filth, wasteth he his time in idle pursuits."

Only if we turn within, as directed by the Master, shall we go beyond pleasure and pain, good and evil. Those who have found the Master, learned the secret and contacted Nam 'within' during their lifetime, are the ones who have truly justified their existence. All praise and honour be to them. "In every heart abideth the Lord; blank is none, but worthy of worship is he, who in himself hath made Him manifest."

The inestimable wealth is within all of us, but can be gathered only after learning the technique from a Perfect Adept and practising it with love, faith and humility. "None is poor, Bhikha; everyone hath got rubies in his bundle. But how to open the knot he doth not know, and therefore is he a pauper." Fortunate indeed are those who have cultivated love for 'Nam' and have turned their back on the world. "All worldly people are prisoners awaiting the stroke of death; save for that rare brave, who hath his body in prison but his soul in heaven."

* * *

17. He Who created the soul and the body resides within each being. He is Eternal and Unchangeable. He can be realized by contacting Nam, which constantly resounds at the eye focus. "Gather the wealth of Nam which none can steal, nor fire can burn, nor even wind can carry. That wealth is never lost." It is the only way to end pain and suffering, and earn lasting bliss.

Everybody is going crazy under the lash of the five passions. They are truly deadly maladies. They destroy by insidious infection and dissolution. Their end is darkness and despair. They make false pretenses and hold out alluring promises. They constantly keep us in the mirage of wealth, lust and pleasures, of power and position, only to lead us headlong into the valley of death. The sole escape from their clutches is through the intervention of a Perfect Adept. He discloses the secret of vacating the 'nine doors' of the body, concentrating the attention in the tenth–at the eye centre – and contacting Nam, the Heavenly Music, hearing which we get rid of all vices and the play of passions.

A life of piety and virtue is possible only when we rise above the 'nine portals' of the body. So long as we remain within their domain and influence, no matter what we do, we cannot conquer the mind and the senses. It is little use cleaning the "utensil again and again if we put nothing into it". The pious life has a meaning only if it can achieve salvation. This can happen only if with the Grace of the Lord, we meet a living Master and learn from Him the technique of contacting Nam. This factor determines whether we take to the path of Kal (the Negative Power) or that of Dayal (the Merciful Lord). Those who go within and develop spiritual vision know that He alone is the Doer, whatever happens is according to His will, and He can be realized only through Guru and Nam.

Such persons who become one with Nam also realize that God resides in everybody. All the different forms are His, even as water, ice and steam are one; but this is clear only to those who have melted ice into water and have heated water into steam. Similarly, those who have merged their attention in Nam realize that He pervades everywhere and that all the external forms and phenomena are His manifestations.

* * *

18. All men are made alike. They have the same origin. The Maker is also one. They are a drop of the same Ocean and have ultimately to return to the same Absolute Reality. The way to return Home and realize Him is within us and is also the same for all. He is Real. He is Eternal. He is Everlasting. Everything in the universe and the universe itself is false. He alone is True (unchangeable).

We cannot realize the Lord through contemplation, even if we adopt this method a million times. He is far above and beyond mind and intellect, both of which are truly blind. They fail to resolve even our worldly predicaments. Neither can He be attained by observing silence, nor by penances, pilgrimages and the like. Mind and its ingenuity fail to point the way, for it is beyond mind's reach. The only way to perceive Him is by resigning to His Will, by obeying the Hukum* and treading the path of Shabd. The Hukum or Shabd is within all of us and can be contacted at the eye focus. "By Hukum all forms are made, by Hukum all living beings are created. By Hukum is greatness achieved. By Hukum are made the high and low. By Hukum are pain and pleasure set down. By Hukum are some pardoned. By Hukum are others made to continue in the eternal wheel. Everyone is within Hukum. Exempt is none. If one understands the Hukum, he will not speak in conceit." Nothing can happen without Hukum. It is all ordained from above. No one can die or be killed, even in the midst of flying bullets, unless it is so destined. Such a realization can, however, come only when one goes within and contacts Shabd.

The 'entrance' to the subtle region lies in the part of our body above the eyes. This indeed is a great mystery, for these realms lie behind the veil of mind and cannot be comprehended on the physical plane of consciousness. The surgeons and the doctors cannot discover them when operating upon the living or dissecting the dead. In order to perceive them, one has to lose consciousness of the outside world, become alive or super-conscious within and contact Nam. The Heavenly Melody is continuously reverberating in the part of the body above the eyes. We do not hear it, because our attention is directed downwards and outwards. "God is calling out to us from the top of this beautiful mansion (the human body)". We cannot understand Sach or Shabd, until our attention returns to its source within. The whole world is spiritually asleep. We become awake when we go in at the eye centre. The sweet Melody is constantly coming there, directly, from the House of God.

When we lose our way in a dense forest on a dark night and are without a guide, we try to listen for some sound so that

---

* Hukum – means 'His Order', 'His will'. It also means 'Shabd'.

we may follow it and reach a habitation. In view of the pitch darkness and the unknown place we also look for a light to enable us to reach the place. Likewise, in our spiritual journey, God has provided Divine Light and Sound to lead us safely Home from this labyrinthine world. "Inside is the Flame and in that Flame is sweet Melody that inspireth in us love for the True Lord." When we carry out the instructions prescribed by the Master with faith and loving devotion, we are soon illuminated inside and contacting Nam, listen to the heavenly music, by following which we reach its source or origin. "By practising Nam, doubts and darkness disappear and the light of a million suns shines forth."

For God-realization, therefore, we must first find a Teacher, learn the secret from Him and then vacate the nine portals of the body in accordance with His instructions. It is impossible to advance even an inch on the spiritual path without the Guide who is well versed in this science. We cannot realize Him by recitals, penances, pilgrimages and charities. These have doubtless their own merit, but are utterly unable to release us from the bondage of birth and death. No man can enter spiritual regions so long as his mind lingers upon things of the outer world. He must go to sleep so far as the things of the world are concerned, and wake up within to attain the subtle ones. True liberation can come only when we learn the way from an Adept and 'go within'. This is the path of all the Saints.

PART III

Excerpts from Letters

Excerpts from letters to seekers and disciples

1948–1951

1. You must all have been deeply grieved at the departure on April second, of our late beloved Master from this physical plane. The Satsang suffers an irreparable loss. The enchanting figure is no longer before our eyes. But the Master never dies. His Radiant Shabd Form is within every one of us. He is functioning from the higher planes and is helping His disciples. They should diligently work upon His instructions and they will find Him within themselves. He has commanded me to be at your service and I will do my best to carry out His command.

* * *

2. Spiritually speaking, the human body may be divided into two parts. One part is from the soles of the feet to the eyes, and the other part is from the eyes up to the top of the head. The lower part, including the eyes, is meant to function in this material world. This is known to common man. But what is not known to most people is that the upper part is meant to connect the soul and the mind with higher regions.

This connection begins at the eye centre, after the soul and the mind have vacated the lower portion by means of Repetition, with the attention fixed at the eye centre. The object of Repetition is to accomplish this. Repetition is not an end in itself, but is the *means* to an end. The Repetition of the five Holy Names takes the mind and the soul to a point which leads to the upper portion. When this point has been gained, the Sound Current lifts the soul towards the top of the head, in order to establish connection with the higher planes.

* * *

3. I am in receipt of your letter and appreciate your sentiments. I am very glad to learn that you realize the nature and significance of the real problem—the temptations of the mind. This is *the* problem. Soul is of the essence of Nam and naturally feels a strong attraction towards its Source or Origin. However, it is held down by the attractions and temptations of the mind, like a gas-filled balloon which is moored to the ground by strings.

You cannot conquer the mind by intellectual reasoning. It can be stilled only by drawing the attention inwards and upwards by means of Simran, which collects all the attention currents at the eye centre. When this course is complete, one is able to contact the Shabd. One can hear it earlier also, but at that stage it does not pull because our consciousness has identified itself with the body. The mind finds the Shabd so attractive and delightful that it does not crave other pleasures. Till this state is reached, one should reason with himself, increase the practice and wean himself away from outward pleasures as far as possible. You cannot go out and go in at the same time.

Other problems should also be attended to in the spirit of duty, and solved in the light of personal knowledge and experience and the advice of friends. For health, the physician should be consulted when necessary, though a good, clean, cheerful and active life automatically makes for good health and happiness.

Faith and love make things easy, especially when they are supported by regular meditation.

Please keep to your meditation periods regularly and, if

you have any difficulties, refer them to this place whenever
you like.

* * *

4. Do your best and leave the rest to God. We are so
hedged in and our so-called free will is so much conditioned
by both, the outside circumstances as well as our inner reflexes,
that it can hardly be called 'free.'

By treating the patients and relieving them of their pain
and disease, the doctors do not lay up bad karmas. By using
aspirin or similar pain-relieving remedies, you do not postpone
the period of suffering to a future date. Yes, it is best to avoid
medicines which contain glandular extracts or other substances
of animal origin.

* * *

5. Man is the top of all creation, the perfect handiwork
of Nature in all respects. He contains within himself the key
to unlock the mystery of the Universe and to contact the Creator.
It is the greatest and the highest good fortune of any sentient
being to be born in the form of man.

But his responsibilities are also correspondingly great.
Having come up to the top of the evolutionary ladder, he should
now step onto the ladder of NAM and tread the Spiritual Path
that will ultimately lead him to the Divine Home whence he
came. If he fails to do so, he slides down and, according to his
karmas, his desires and inclinations, he will have to sojourn in
this world of change and go through the various forms of
creation.

In the human body, the eye centre is the spot which
represents the end of one course and the beginning of the
other. Man may go up or he may slide down.

This is the message which all Saints and Masters have
given to the world, in their own time. Our dearly beloved
Master, Baba Sawan Singh Ji, in whose memory we have

gathered here today, preached this very Truth for forty-five years. He helped those who accepted His teachings and is indeed helping all of us still, and I can do no better than to call your attention to this vital message of our Great Master.

* * *

6. The first step towards Spiritual practice is to understand the object of hearing the Shabd. The function of Shabd is to lift the soul upwards and inwards, to the higher planes. But the Shabd is unable to lift the soul so long as it is not withdrawn from the entire body and collect in the eye focus. Just as a fine piece of cloth, which is entangled in a thorny bush, is torn to shreds if one tries to pull it up forcibly, without first disengaging it from each thorn, similarly the Shabd would not lift the soul up so long as it is permeating every pore of the body, though the Sound may be audible.

Therefore, the first step is to withdraw the attention currents from the body up to the point where the Sound can lift it. This is brought about by concentration of the attention in the eye centre, which is possible only when the mind becomes motionless. There are various methods for making the mind motionless and for collecting the attention currents in the eyes. But the simplest and the easiest of them all is the Repetition of the Holy Names prescribed by the Saints, while the attention is fixed between the eyes. In fact, it is the mind that does the repeating.

It is not an easy matter to bring the mind under control and to make it tranquil and motionless. It requires years of patient labour. When concentration is complete and the soul currents have been withdrawn up to the eye centre, the attention should be kept up there with the help of Dhyan, which is contemplation on the Radiant Form of the Master.

* * *

7. The attention currents should be collected into the

eye focus. The attention should be fixed at the place between and above the eyes, where one ordinarily keeps the attention when thinking. The bell sound does not lift the soul until the attention currents from the entire body have been collected in the eye focus.

* * *

8.   The message of the Masters is natural, not artificial. The entire Macrocosm is within the human body, which is therefore called the Microcosm. The only way to study the Macrocosm is through the Microcosm. Christ called the human body "the temple of the living God" for the same reason. Not only the creation, but God, the Creator, also lives within man and can be met within this temple. The result is that the Spiritual journey from this material plane to the highest plane of pure spirit lies within the human body. It begins from the toes of the feet and ends at the top of head.

This journey is divided into two parts: The first part is from the feet to the eye centre. It consists of concentrating the mind and making the attention stay at the eye centre, so that the attention currents are withdrawn from the entire lower portion of the body into the eye centre. The second part is from the eye centre to the top of the head. Here the concentrated soul is able to catch the Sound Current which descends from the top of the head to the eye centre. The soul is gradually lifted up from the eye centre to the top of the head by means of the Sound Current.

We pass through five vast planes in the course of this journey. The Sound Current is one and the same, but in passing through the different regions it assumes different aspects. The method of the Sound Current is complete while all other courses, such as Pranayam, Mudra, etc., are incomplete.

If, during our lifetime, we travel the path which we have to traverse after death, then death loses its terror for us. It is the object and goal of human life to take the soul to the region whence it originally descended. Thus the soul is liberated from the cycle of births and deaths.

* * *

9.   As you proceed with your meditation, you will feel peace and bliss, but it should be a lasting and not a momentary feeling. This will come when you have practiced and devoted considerable time to the Sound Current. Sanskaras, *i.e.,* impressions of past lives, enable some people to hear the Sound easily, but to hear alone is not enough. You must be one with it. Your love for the Master and the repetition of the Holy Names enables you to do this. There is power, happiness and bliss in Nam, also called the Word, Shabd or the Sound. And the real form of the Master is also Shabd. It is *That* which we all seek.

The service which we value and appreciate most is that which helps the disciple, and that is 'Surat-Shabd' service, or devotion to the Sound Current. It is good to be helpful to others, but to be able to render proper and effective help to others in their spiritual uplift, one must first of all be in a position to do so, *i.e.,* he should have worked his way up sufficiently for this purpose.

Nothing should stand in the way of your meditation, and no disciple should plunge so deep into worldly affairs as to enable them to interfere with his Bhajan or affect his mental poise.

* * *

10.   I want you to progress still further on the spiritual journey. Increase the concentration of your mind, and take your soul to the portal which opens into the astral plane, after vacating the entire body. The Master's astral form can be contacted at this gate. He will talk to you and reply to all your questions. You say that you had contacted the late Master in a past birth, but it is clear that you did not gain the higher planes then; otherwise it would not have been necessary for you to undergo the pangs of rebirth into this physical world. I wish that you try your best to reach the Spiritual Region during this life, so that you may not have to come here again. Please devote as much time as you can to spiritual practice. Your spiritual progress will be helpful to your deceased mother also.

There are very few real seekers after Truth, and fewer still who can conform to the restrictions prescribed for spiritual progress. Therefore, working hard for your own spiritual progress should be your primary object. Besides the regular time, almost the whole of your spare time and attention should be given to that end. Much time should not be wasted in "helping" others. If you find anyone keenly interested and prepared to conform to the mode of life of follower of Radha Soami, you may lend him books and refer him to me.

* * *

11.   The Creator Himself is within us, including all that He has created in the material, mental and spiritual regions. As the spirit is drawn up higher and higher, things will be clearer, and the how and why of things also will become intelligible. This world is only a projection of the mental world. And whoever has studied and explored the mental world automatically knows this world too, infinitely better.

Sant Mat does not enslave, but teaches the disciple to be really independent by means of self-control and self-knowledge.

————Such things are usual with one who goes in, but the knowledge or information should not be given out. It is seldom valued properly by others, and you really suffer a loss. Silence is a great virtue.

* * *

12.   A Satsangi should not court worldly pleasures. In

fact, he should avoid them as far as possible. When a patient takes a doctor's medicine, he also has to follow his instructions regarding diet, etc., and abstain from things which he has been asked to cut out. Likewise, a Satsangi should follow the other instructions along with meditation.

In the beginning, the disciple still feels the attraction of wordly pleasures and glamour, although he resists them. He pays attention only to the things which are necessary and rejects the others. Then comes a stage in his progress when he has contacted Nam within, and he enjoys the spiritual delights. In comparison with *That*, the worldly pleasures are uninteresting and meaningless, and have no appeal for him. He uses the world, but is not attracted by it.

As for books, they are good to read, enjoy and confirm your inner experiences, but they cannot *take* you in.

* * *

13. Many religions take Brahm as the highest spiritual region and the Creator of all. Their inquiry is incomplete and limited. Brahm is not the maker of all creation. His creation and rulership extend to the second stage only, and herein also he can neither create nor destroy souls. All that he does is to keep the souls confined within his domain by putting them in physical, astral and causal bodies, frames or cages. He thereby makes them forget their origin or Home, which is in the fifth stage. Transmigration according to the law of Karma is the system of his government. Birth and decay, and the dualism of good and evil, pleasure and pain are the order of his domain.

Most religions in the world have been promulgated by Brahm and they aim at keeping order in this creation. Brahm does not want a single soul to get even an inkling of what lies beyond him. Through the agency of revealed books, prophets and incarnations, he makes himself known as the highest spiritual stage of development and the maker of all creation, and his law as infallible.

To confound people and to entangle them in the karmic complications, nothing beats meat eating and the use of intoxicants—particularly alcohol,—and nothing appeals to people faster than a show of miracles. Therefore, the prophets and incarnations of Brahm generally take a lenient view against the use of liquor and we quite often find them permitting such things. The lower the stage of the prophet, the greater the freedom allowed in the use of these things.

The work of the prophets and incarnations of Brahm is to see that the creation in his charge remains intact and confined within his sphere, and that no one deserts it by going to real spiritual regions which are beyond Brahm. On the other hand, the work of the Saints is to free the souls, which are imprisoned by Brahm, and take them to their Spiritual Home of Eternal Bliss. The Saints positively prohibit the use of meat and liquor, and they also discourage the performance of miracles, as that is against the laws of Nature. These three acts are strong barriers, par excellence, which stand in the way of crossing the boundary of Brahm.

* * *

14.   The usual procedure for every individual after death, is that he is taken to the court of Dharam Rai to render an account of his karmas. Jesus says that people will have to render account "to the utmost farthing." In some cases, however, there is an interval between death here and their appearance before Dharam Rai. Some good, clean souls, after death and before appearing in the court for rendering account and returning to this world, go to higher regions within the sphere of Brahm to enjoy the fruits of their good actions. Similarly, very dirty souls, after death and before rendering account and coming back to this world, suffer for their evil deeds in the form of ghosts and goblins in sub-astral regions.

Both of these conditions may be taken as a continuity of their lives here.

* * *

15. A very important though ordinarily unknown factor—we might call it X—in these matters is the influence of one's past karmas and past achievements.

The sufferings of good men with evolved minds is not inexplicable. They have surely been very good and have done nothing in this life to merit such suffering, but what about the past—about that unknown factor ? Only those who 'go in' sufficiently can see the cause. And, again, our present life is already determined before we are born. All human beings have necessarily to get their share of good and bad karmas for, if their karmas were all good, they would be somewhere on the astral plane and, if wholly bad, they would be sub-human.

Sant Mat, however, does not teach us to get away from the world, but to rise above it. Outwardly, one should be in the world, but inwardly, away from it.

* * *

16. Thank you for your letter offering me wholehearted devotion and co-operation.

Not only all true Masters are one in Shabd, but also all human beings are one in Shabd. The only difference is that the Masters have realized the Truth within themselves and have become one with the Shabd, and one with each other. Other human beings have not realized the Truth.

My only wish is that you try to contact the Radiant Form of the Master within you, so that you may become sure by actual experience of the great Truth taught by the Master. This is the greatest service that a disciple can render to his Master. All other services—that of body, mind and wealth—are subservient to this great objective and should lead to it. Please accept this short note in reply.

* * *

17. Masters are able to carry on the functions of the body and their daily routine in the world by means of the diffused Spirituality, while their spirit remains and works in higher planes.

* * *

18. A man who has derived benefit from a Master should be full of gratitude and love for Him and should feel proud in proclaiming his Master's Name. In the teachings of the Guru Granth Sahib, it is a sin to conceal one's Master. This attitude of concealment often arises from the consciousness of fear of losing one's reputation or prestige.

Not only in America but also in India and everywhere else it is easier to preach than to practise. It is not an easy matter to act upon the teachings of the Masters. That is why the teachings are apt to be forgotten and misrepresented after the Masters have departed. Instead of practising those teachings, the followers begin to issue commentaries and wrangle about them. Yet that does not mean that we should not treat that person with the respect and consideration due to a religious preacher.

* * *

19. It is true that there is only one Giver and He gives to whomsoever He likes. The wind of Heaven bloweth where it listeth. It is equally correct that humility is the true sign of greatness. We have a proverb that the branches of a tree laden with fruit bend low. So it is with the truly great.

I have read the enclosed literature about–. You may, if you feel like it, take some to supplement your food. But in spite of the great strides that science has made and the wonderful achievements of the science of nutrition, some unknown factor always seems to crop up just when we think we know everything. On the one hand there is the cry 'Back to Nature' and on the other, scientific knowledge isolates nutritional factors, prepares them synthetically and makes us artificial. Can't we agree with the poet when he says, "tis folly to be wise where ignorance is bliss !".

* * *

20.   Let the dying year with all its memories and regrets, pleasant and unpleasant, bring home to us Satsangis the impermanence and unreality of what we behold, and strengthen our resolve to rise above the phenomenal existence and reach the glories of the Word, the Nam that was, is, and will be.

The soul is of the same essence as Nam, and will enjoy real bliss only when it reaches the region of Nam and becomes one with Nam. You have been initiated into this mystery. It behoves you, therefore, to travel the Path as far as possible, for this is the only thing that really matters. But we are not to neglect our worldly duties. With a heart full of love and faith, devote yourself to the task. Also discharge your worldly obligations. With this motto as your guiding principle, may the New Year bring you success and happiness.

* * *

21.   What you say is all the result of your love and faith, and this is a very important factor in successful meditation.

There is no alternative to concentrating your attention at the eye centre and then going up with the aid of Shabd or Sound Current, unless it be wandering about in various forms in this phenomenal world. As long as man is tied to himself, he is tied to the world. When he rises above the nine doors of the body and frees himself from the bodily or sense relations, which he will do when he will completely vacate the body and concentrate all his attention at the eye centre, he is freed from all ties and the world.

The path of the Shabd is the highest and the complete path available to humanity. All others are incomplete in comparison, and it is our duty to tread the path firmly and devotedly.

* * *

22. It is wrong to use violence of any sort. Sant Mat is based upon love and sympathy. Persuasion may be used, but violence never. Soami Ji says : "All those who understood the teachings and acted upon them crossed over with the Master."

The object of Satsang is to draw attention to the weaknesses and to uplift the disciples mentally and spiritually. If the disciple does not utilize his opportunities and does not labour on the Path, he will naturally remain a slave to the mind and the senses, and will come to grief. When in trouble, he will sooner or later turn in and begin his Bhajan, for the inner pull is always there—though the Fate Karma, the Pralabdh, also has to be gone through. But Saints exercise 'Mauj' unfailingly at the time of death. If before that they shower their grace upon one who is still ruled by the pleasures of the senses, so much so that the soul is held fast and cannot rise above them, he cannot profit by the Grace, and the Daya (Mercy) is also wasted.

Your reply is very apt. You grasp the significance and the essence of Sant Mat. Hold fast to it and keep happy. Arguments and discussions seldom bring conviction, and partisans would never be convinced. Why waste time ?

When a disciple, whether initiated in Sound or not [1], hears the Sound, he should look upon it as a mark of the Master's Grace and try all the more to withdraw his consciousness so that he may hear it better.

* * *

23. Whether it is Repetition of the Names or meditation at the eye centre, or attending to the Sound within, all three lead the same way and point to the same goal. I am writing to— also on the subject. We have to leave plurality and come into unity, and should therefore not encourage plurality. Of course, the best way to achieve unity is to leave this material cage, the

---

1. During Maharaj Jagat Singh's period, at the time of initiation, sometimes the seekers were taught only the technique of simran or repetition; Shabd was imparted to them after a few months.

body, and come to the centre behind the eyes.

Let not the organization smother the spirit. Otherwise, people may come to you for worldly help instead of spiritual help, and it may become like a church, an organization for helping the people in their worldly difficulties, or a society in which the rich members help the poor. I would suggest that you confine yourself to spiritual work, helping individuals when necessary and keeping organization in the background. There should be no building, no office, etc. Please do not mix Parmarth (spiritual work) with Swarath (worldly work). Take care of the spirit and other things will take care of themselves.

When our Master was urged to permit the opening of a girls' school here, He said that He would not countenance any school other than the spiritual school. Going in, contacting the Sound Current and starting the upward spiritual journey is the greatest good that you can do to yourself and to others. And whatever stands in the way of your accomplishing this task should be rejected.

* * *

24. I look upon all people travelling the Radha Soami Path as my fellow pupils and regard them as my brothers and sisters. If they are younger, I call them my daughters and sons.

The soul and the mind currents which are permeating every pore of the body, should be collected in the eye centre by means of Repetition of the Holy Names. This is essentially a slow process. One is apt to expect quick results. It involves the labour of years to vacate the entire body below the eyes and to collect the attention and hold it at the eye focus. When this is the case, the body below the eyes feels numb and senseless, but one is conscious within, sees the light and hears the Sound clearly. Before that, the Sound is heard but it does not pull the soul. Therefore, the primary object should be to vacate the body by means of Repetition, and in doing Repetition you should not try to hear the Sound. That would divide the attention.

Do not strain your muscles or attention to catch the Sound. The Sound will come of Itself and will become clearer as the concentration grows deeper.

Let all your efforts be directed towards increasing the concentration. The Master is inside and He tries at times to catch our attention by His voice or by giving us glimpses of His astral form. That is a sign of His mercy and grace, for by showing Himself and by talking to us, He tries to encourage us in our practice.

* * *

25. I am sorry to note that a fellow disciple should have broken his word to you. It is probable that in the beginning the intention was honest. This is the most charitable view of the matter. Of course, you are the best judge. All disciples are not alike and you should remain on your guard. It so happens that the zeal of most of the disciples everywhere is liable to cool down, as success in the Spiritual Practice and concentration is difficult to attain without hard labour and pure living, in which many of them fail miserably. It is a life-long, uphill task. Without successful meditation, few can keep up the zeal and ardour, which they show in the beginning.

I am sorry to know of the hard life you have had to lead, but adverse or easy circumstances in life depend upon past karma, which should be borne patiently and resignedly. In future, only good actions should be performed to avoid creating bad karma. And there is no better action than that of listening to the Sound Current, for this cuts at the root of karma and frees us from the karmic tangle.

Everyone is helpless, however good he may be. He has to bear the consequences of past karma, but is free to sow good seeds for the future. Performing Repetition and listening to the Sound Current is making the best use of one's life on this earth. Therefore, you should try to do your utmost in the circumstances in which you are placed, and devote as much time as you can to your meditation.

The confusion of mind and brain is not the result of meditation.—It is possible that the mind goes out during Repetition, and on account of worldly worries and difficulties, the mind does not stick to Repetition but confuses the brain by generating external thoughts. It should be kept quiet and peaceful at all times, and at least during meditation. I know that the struggle is very hard, especially for one placed in your circumstances; still we are born for struggle in this world, and it is brave not to lose heart. There is no other way out. While living and struggling with the difficulties of this external world, a disciple has to fight with his mind and bring it under control by making it motionless.

Regarding worldly relationship, it may be pointed out that all relationships are based on selfish motives on this material plane. Husbands, brothers, wives, sisters, other relatives and friends are attached to us because of the advantages that accrue to them from us, and are apt to cool down in their zeal and love towards us when they feel that we are of no use to them. Do not expect much from them, but do your duty towards them and care for them, even if they fail to reciprocate your love. This should be the case especially in your relation with your husband. Love and obey him and try to be useful to him. Win over his heart with your love and service.

The Master is always within you in His astral and Shabd forms, and is watching over you. Please do not despair. Turn your thoughts to Him during your times of difficulty and trouble. Derive satisfaction from the knowledge that the burden of your karma is being lightened day by day, by undergoing and facing the difficulties of your life.

* * *

26. You are always free to write whenever you feel like

it. Regarding your visit to — and the disappointing results, it was certainly your karmas which took you to that place. When the time for the fruition of karma arrives, the intellect is biased in favour of that particular course of action.

I would only say this much: judge things from the worldly point of view, take business advice; then go into meditation, think of the Master and act. Please do your Bhajan and Simran regularly, so that you may have peace and feel the grace of the Master.

* * *

27.   Thank you for your letter describing the details of your meditative exercises. Your ardour and love for the Spiritual Path have borne fruit and you have got the way which you are now treading, but it is a long and weary way, especially in its initial stages. It has been described as "the way of the ant," which slowly and laboriously selects the grains of sugar from the grains of sand with which it is mixed. The Shabd pervades everywhere, and when you are fully in contact with the Shabd or Sound Current in the eye centre, and the concentration is complete, then you are able to separate the Vital Power from the material, just as the ant separates the sugar from the sand.

You may certainly communicate your experiences and your difficulties. The Masters know, but seldom take the initiative on what They know inwardly.

I am glad to read of your experiences and congratulate you on your persistence. This is the essence of the thing, as it were. You have yourself seen that the next time it was far less painful and you practically won the struggle. It is natural that one should feel some pain when the spirit current is first withdrawn sufficiently to cause the lower body to become numb. But once this has been overcome by determination, the task becomes comparatively easier. The pressure, the strain, the difficulty in breathing, the facial spasm, are all indications of a struggle that happily seems to be almost over. Concentrate on the Repetition of the Sacred Names, with the attention centered at the eye focus, and when that is complete, the struggle will be won. You need not entertain fear of any trouble, disability or death occuring during meditation.

Yes, the concentration will go on improving if you repeat the Holy Names lovingly and steadfastly. Short periods of meditation of at least one-half hour each, in addition to the usual regular periods, are helpful and you may utilize such intervals.

To practise meditation at a time when the stomach is empty and the food has been digested is decidedly better.

You need not talk to others about this Path, which is new to you, until you have gained a surer footing and richer experiences. Your life, your mental poise and your behaviour will automatically impress others, and they will themselves wonder and inquire as to what has brought about the change.

* * *

28. Magic, spiritualism and all such practices are antagonistic to the Radha Soami Path. Anyone who indulges in them cannot expect to make progress in concentration and meditation. No such person can get Initiation unless and until he gives up such pursuits. Also, any disciple who wishes to make spiritual progress will have to severe connections with all those who practice black magic, spiritualism and the like.

You should go on giving time to your Repetition and Concentration. Then no evil influence can touch you.

* * *

29. You say that your zeal for the practice of meditation has been weak, because the desired results have not been forthcoming. You were Initiated about five years ago. An Initiate is expected to devote a minimum of two and a half hours every day to his devotions. If you had given so much time daily, even to Repetition alone, the mind would have been stilled.

The first step is to make the mind motionless by means of Repetition, with the attention fixed at the eye centre. During numerous past births, the mind has acquired the habit of wandering out. It is not still for even a moment. Constant and concerted labour is required for many years to make the mind motionless. Unless the mind is still, it cannot go in.

The reason for your inability to go in is not vasectomy, but the lack of regular and continuous practice of Repetition. If you want results, you should devote at least two hours daily to Repetition with attention, and half an hour to the listening of the Sound Current, regularly. There is no simpler and surer method than this.

Mind is not an ordinary power that will easily submit to our control. It rules the world. So long as our attention is confined within the nine portals of the body, it is out of control. Our control over the mind increases in juxtaposition to the withdrawal of the currents from the extremities of the body, towards the eye centre. When the withdrawal is complete and the mind comes under control, the attention is held at the eye centre and is able to take full advantage of the Sound Current by rising and riding on It.

* * *

30.   I may tell you at once, however, that such practices are not countenanced by Satsang, in any way.—is expected to know the principles of Sant Mat. There is a still more important point to note and that is that *no* black magic, charm or such practices can in any way affect Satsangis. All that they have to do is to repeat the five Holy Names—with confidence and love—and the evil influence, if any, dare not approach them. Of course, the more regularly and lovingly you perform your Repetition, the more effective is your defense and protection.

Sant Mat is the religion of love and persuasion, and not of force or coercion. It is also wrong to suppose that the Master does not care how we live or what we do if only we go on doing our meditation. To begin with, progress in spiritual meditation is, to a great extent, dependent on our life and thoughts, which are an integral part of the discipline. It would benefit her considerably if she were to devote all her attention to meditation and not think of other things too much.

There is no use in rendering service which is not liked and appreciated. Besides, when children grow up, they change a good deal and it is neither possible nor desirable that they should be forced or coerced. It is we grown-ups who should fit in with the changed conditions.

You should also devote the maximum time that you can, and certainly not less than two and one-half hours every day, to the Spiritual exercises (two hours to Repetition of the Holy Names and one-half hour to hearing the internal Sound). If you do that regularly and lovingly, the situation will improve.

* * *

31. I am in receipt of your letter and have read, with interest, the description of your vision and experience. These are encouragements on the Path and should induce you to give more time to meditation, and make you practice even more devotedly. As you do so, you will see and hear many things.

You do the right thing in minding the Sound when concentrating on the increasing light. The Sound is always there and it is a good thing that the Bell Sound comes to you also while going about your work, but you should pay attention to it only when it comes from the right ear or the forehead. It should be ignored when it comes from the left ear. You should attend to no sound, not even the bell sound, when it emanates from the left.

* * *

32. You are old disciples and know the principles which

should govern the conduct of Radha Soami disciples. Our main business is to go in, contact the Sound Current and thus rise above the struggles of this world. The world is a cockpit. It has never been, nor is, nor shall ever be at peace. Struggle is a characteristic of this world, and it is hard, very hard, to face it.

Those who go in and contact Nam, rise above the struggle and come to dwell in the land of peace and happiness. Those who remain struggling in this phenomenal world, will continue to be a part of this changing world and will be born again and again, in various forms and under various circumstances, to fulfil their desires.

However, we have to do our duties and discharge our obligations to the country and society in which we live, but in a spirit of duty and detachment. The advice given to you by our Great Master holds good and is the golden rule. "There can be no harm in joining a society which aims at social uplift, etc., if it does not absorb too much time or if it provides a means of livelihood. Only so much time should be devoted to worldly or other work as is necessary to keep it going." You may continue to be members, but it should not absorb too much of your time and should not interfere with your Bhajan. This is the test. Do your duty but do not get entangled in programmes and organizations. Salvation is an individual problem and there is only one way to it, *i.e.,* by going in and contacting Nam.

* * *

33. I am glad that you appreciate the value of Initiation, but the real appreciation comes only when by Simran (Repetition of the Holy Names) you vacate the body and go in. It is then that you will know what it is to have a Master and you will see for yourself what He does for His disciples. The real aim of Initiation is to go in and contact the Master; then, with His help, and under His guidance, to complete our Spiritual

Journey, which begins from the toes and ends at the top of the head.

You need not be sorry for being late in joining the Satsang. There is a time for everything, but now the harmony of the family circle is complete. You should try to sit together for Satsang, if it is possible to do so without interfering with your duties.

As for other things, try your best and then do not worry, for whatever follows will be for your ultimate benefit. With faith and confidence in your heart, forge ahead materially as well as spiritually.

* * *

34. It has given me a genuine pleasure to learn of your happy family life and loving marital relations. This is as it should be.

Hard work does make one feel tired and sometimes sleepy, for sleep is nature's mode of giving rest to the body. At such times, it is difficult to meditate properly, but one can keep the thoughts on the Master, *i.e.,* inwardly dwell on the Master and Shabd.

Please try to find time for Bhajan when your mind is fresh and the body is less tired. If you can manage it, early morning after you have had your full sleep, is very good. The meditation that you do now is doubly useful, for it will influence the mentality of the child and will plant good Sanskaras—prenatal impressions—on the child. Your thinking of the Master and reading good books, either Satsang literature or other good moral books, will have the same effect.

* * *

35. The importance of a living Master, as you say, is great, particularly in Sant Mat. Our Great Master, Baba Sawan Singh Ji who Initiated you—shook off His mortal coil on

April 2, 1948, as you have already been informed—and since then, according to His express command as embodied in His Last Will, I am carrying on His work.

It is not every day that such Great Masters come to the world. His reach was immense and His Spiritual Power immeasurable. Even this short period is enough. He supervises and takes a kindly paternal interest in His struggling children, and can be contacted by such of His disciples who, by intensive Bhajan and Simran and love for Him, are able to go in.

I shall be happy to answer any questions you may like to ask, and render whatever help is possible on the Path.

Saints are Shabd or Nam personified—'the WORD made flesh'—and if you can withdraw your mind from the world and its attractions, go in and contact Nam, you can be in touch with the Master. Nam pervades everywhere and in you, and it is there, within yourself, that you may contact It.

* * *

36. Very pleased to hear from you and to learn from your letter that things have improved so well and that your path has been smoothened by the Great Master. The Inner Power is unerring and, if only the disciple has enough faith and love, the response is always there. All things come to him who does his duty and waits in love and faith. I am so glad that your home life has improved and that you have also now got work.

The experience that you have passed through is also very good and is a sign that the hold of the Negative Power is loosening.

* * *

37. Pran Yoga or Pranayam, is an artificial method. It aims at control of mind through the control of breath. At death, Pran is left behind and, with it, the means of controlling the mind. It is like putting chains on a bad character. So long as the chains are holding him, he behaves all right; but as soon as the chains are removed, the bad character resumes his old evil ways. Moreover, Pran Yoga involves danger to health and that is also why the Masters do not approve of this method. The method of the Saints is natural. They want to control and concentrate the mind by means of Repetition, while the attention is fixed at the eye centre. By constant and regular practice, the attention currents begin to concentrate and the body begins to be vacated from the extremities upwards until the whole body becomes numb and all the soul and mind currents are concentrated in the third eye. And when the Sound Current is contacted, the mind comes under control forever.

No doubt yogis are earnest and sincere, but that does not affect the method they prescribe. The purpose of life is to bring about complete concentration of mind and thereby vacate the entire body. Precisely the same thing happens at death. This is technically known as "separating the animate from the inanimate." The method of Repetition should not cause pain anywhere in the body, after the period of meditation. If there is any pain, a doctor should be consulted. You should read all the available literature on this Path.

You should not be anxious about other seekers. God, who is their Maker, will look after them. You should care for your own Spiritual advancement. Yes, you may meet the followers of the Masters, who are themselves engaged in the practice of Repetition. Their society will counteract the influence of the other school. Also read books on the path, to give strength to your conviction. In India too, all the people do not realize the purpose of life, and it is only very few who follow the teachings of the Master.

Do not try to catch the Sound. Try to bring about concentration by means of Repetition. When the concentration grows, the Sound will come of itself.

* * *

38. You may write to me freely about your progress as well as your difficulties. Meditation is a mental process, and if one can take the attention in at any time, it is easily done. Regularity of time, seclusion and adoption of certain postures are aids to the process of concentration, and are very desirable because they prevent the attention from being distracted. But if it is not possible to keep certain hours, meditation and concentration may be practiced in any posture and at any time which is convenient to you. Likewise Simran or the Repetition of the Holy Names can be practiced quietly, especially when one has leisure.

It is good that you occasionally feel the proximity of the Master. This is the result of your faith and love, and your devotion to your Spiritual duty.

For your physical ailment, it is right to contact a doctor and follow his advice.

* * *

39. I also note your difficulty regarding the sex problem. You have been in the army and may be said to be a technical man. You would do well to grasp the technical connection between the mind and the body. The object of Initiation is to enable the disciple to concentrate all his attention and consciousness at the eye centre (the thinking centre), so that he may be able to contact the Shabd, the Divine Melody which is resounding within and, with Its help, go up and reach the highest Spiritual Region whence it emanates.

As long as the mind is attached to outward forms and is ruled by the sense pleasures, it cannot go up to the thinking centre. Yielding to the senses also weakens the intrinsic power of the mind, for then it has to depend for its pleasure and enjoyment on external objects instead of upon itself. Forms change and their pleasures also are short-lived, besides occasionally giving one a severe shock. If man were to make himself independent of outward forms and seek happiness and enjoyment within, he would grow strong and be able to go in at will. Then he would shed all his weaknesses and hold the mind and senses in control.

Lust is perhaps the strongest of the five deadly enemies and must be fought. Adding fuel to the fire only increases the conflagration and certainly does not extinguish it. I would suggest that you control it consciously:

   (a)   by dwelling upon its harmful effects.
   (b)   by developing the opposite qualities, *i.e.,* controlled and virtuous life, and realizing the immense help it gives in spiritual life.
   (c)   by keeping yourself busy with your duties.

When means and circumstances permit, you may marry and settle down, and lead a controlled married life.

* * *

40.   You now have the technique for meditation and you should find regular time for it every day. If you cannot sit for two and a half hours at a time, you should sit as long as you conveniently can and then increase the period gradually. If pressed too much for time you may divide it into two periods, but it is always preferable to have one long sitting. The important thing is to withdraw the current of consciousness from the body and hold it at the eye centre.

Your being an Initiate should make you a more loving son than before. You should never try to force your views on them but should win them over by your conduct, and if you are true to your spiritual duties, it is bound to influence them.

* * *

41.   We go to different places mostly to finish up our karmas and square up our accounts, so you need not be very sorry for your coming to——but look upon it as one of the phases of your life. It is good that things now wear a better look.

Please try to find a better house and, till you get another, try to make yourself as comfortable as you can under the circumstances. One should strive, but without being affected by the results.

Above all, do not miss your Bhajan and Simran. Attend to it regularly please and also look after your worldly interests, and the Master will bless you. But please remember that your spiritual duties are not to be neglected under any circumstance.

* * *

42.   I am sorry to learn of your financial and other troubles but I may at once tell you that black magic will not touch you if you are true to your pledges as a Satsangi and do you Repetition of Names properly. Black magic affects only weak-willed people. Even non-Satsangis cannot be affected by it if they possess a strong will.

Troubles and disappointments and even failures do come to us in life. We should face them with a strong will and with faith and confidence in the Master. You have been taught to rise above these distractions by faithful and regular Repetition of the Sacred Names. Similarly, when you fear adverse influences, you should not think of them but of the Master and Nam and try to take your attention to the eye centre with quiet mental Repetition of the five Holy Names given to you at the time of Initiation.

As for your relations with your wife, I would advise you to bear with her patiently. You may be able to convert her by love, forbearance and tolerance but not by petulance and peevishness or disagreement. If she or other people criticize the Faith, you should not get offended for they are uninstructed and ignorant, but you are the knowing one. If better and more

harmonious relations are established between you and your
wife, not only would you be happier but——.

Pray inwardly to the Master and then with a kindly and
hopeful heart do what you think is right to meet the situation,
and please remember that all things are not settled by argument.
A spirit of mutual accommodation is far more helpful than
cold logic.

* * *

43. It is true that there is no happiness in this world. We
get only temporary satisfaction. Soon we get fed up and turn
elsewhere, but with the same result. Happiness comes by going
in and contacting Nam because there is no change in the regions
of pure Spirit or Nam. The phenomenal world is the world of
change and the spiritual world is the world of Eternal Bliss.
The way to it lies within you.

By concentration and repetition of the five Names you
have to withdraw the current of consciousness that now
pervades the entire body, up to the eye centre and thence catch
the Sound Current. If you devote yourself earnestly to this
task, you will hardly have much time for other things, and your
desire for over indulgence will automatically vanish. You have
tried so many things. Now try this also in right earnest and see
the result.

* * *

44. In the first place I shall strongly advise you and, in
fact, all the followers of Radha Soami to cleanse their minds
of all superstition and superstitious suspicions. Please
remember that our troubles in this life are due to our actions,
past and present, and that no one has any power to do us any
sort of harm by his so-called magic influence. R.S. followers
should have a stronger mind than to attribute their troubles to
'evil influence' of others.

Everyone is accountable for his own actions. The wife will not be held responsible for her husband's actions and the husband will not have to suffer for the shortcomings of his wife. Each one will have to undergo the result of his or her own actions. Therefore, if anyone does not conform to the vegetarian diet, it is he alone who will have to suffer for the delinquency. Radha Soami does not impose this diet for the sake of form. He warns everyone, whether he be a follower of Radha Soami or not, that a flesh-eater or winebibber will have to suffer. Those who do not heed this warning, will have to account for it.

* * *

45.   I am glad to learn that you now feel better. If we do our part faithfully, help is always vouchsafed. Help is, in fact, always given but we cannot know and realize it unless we go in. It is *then* that we really feel that our doubts are being settled. I would appreciate your giving proper time to meditation. Think of worldly business when due, but also find time for the most important business of life. Out of twenty-four hours we are enjoined to devote only two and one-half hours, and if circumstances be unfavourable and we cannot find two and one-half hours at a time, we are allowed the concession of completing this quota in two or three instalments.

Our true mission in life is to withdraw our attention to the eye centre and contact Nam, and thereby become supermen, but we are not to neglect our worldly duties and should earn our living in an honest manner by following whatever trade or profession we are fit for or can take to easily. A life of spiritual meditation does not mean a life of sloth or haphazard careering. We should work with a determined will in both spheres.

* * *

46.   The deep longings that you cherish and the thoughts about the Radha Soami faith becoming prevalent in your country that are constantly with you, are indications of your good Sanskaras or past impressions. You want to share the good things with your countrymen. It all depends upon their Karma and His Grace. It is certainly not impossible. Such thoughts have a chastening and purifying influence on the mind.

It may not be possible for you to come here physically, but in thought and spirit you can, by devoting yourselves to Repetition of the Holy Names and listening to the Sound Current. The Sound Current is ubiquitous, pervades everywhere and receives the messages of loving hearts. Those who are in tune with It, feel Its presence. It is a question of tuning in, like the radio.

* * *

47. Ups and downs in business and in most things in life are natural, but worry never helped anybody. The proper thing is to handle the situation in the light of your experience and worldly wisdom and with faith and hope.

To be helpful and selfless is certainly good, but we should not identify ourselves with such work. We should help in a detached spirit and to the extent that it does not constitute a burden on our minds. Perform your social duties and discharge your obligations, but do not neglect your own proper work which is that of going 'in'. In other words, do not get entangled. The one unfailing test in all such matters is, "Does it interfere with my Bhajan ?" If it does, discard it unhesitatingly.

Before sitting down, clear your mind of all thoughts, then do your Simran (Repetition of the five Holy Names) with love and faith. If thoughts of business or other worries interfere during your meditation period, suggest to yourself quietly but firmly that you will attend to them afterwards and not now.

* * *

48.   Thank you for the appreciation of the Master's help. He does what He thinks proper. If we do our duty, why would He not do His? We should proceed in love and faith and see that we do not transgress His commandments. The best and most appropriate way of appreciating His kindness and expressing our gratitude is to give more and more time to Bhajan and Simran, so that we may go in and contact Nam, and thus have a first hand experience of everything.

* * *

49.   Am glad to know that you appreciate the privilege of Initiation and are putting in the regular hours of meditation. It is, however, a very slow process, except in the case of those who have trodden the Path in a previous incarnation. You should not expect results too soon. Slow and steady wins the race. Also, what is achieved and consolidated gradually is lasting. The more effort you put in, the more will you make things easier, not only for yourself but for your wife also.

* * *

50.   The real appreciation comes when one is able to vacate the body, 'go in' and contact Nam.

You may change your residence if it suits you. As to diet, simple, easily digestible vegetarian food is all that is required. If you like uncooked food and it suits you better, you may adopt it. The important point is to withdraw your attention and concentrate it at the eye centre. It is not accomplished in a day, of course; but everything becomes easy by practice. Regarding benevolence and development of other fine traits of character, when you devote yourself to meditation and Nam, these things will come automatically.

* * *

51.   I am sorry to hear about your long illness but, as you seem to realize yourself, you are paying off your karmic debt.

However, this does not mean that you should not have recourse to treatment. On the other hand, you should do all in your power to combat disease and recover health, leaving the result to the Master. Physical pain is compelling and disturbing, no doubt, but the *habit* of Simran at the eye centre makes you indifferent to pain to a very great extent.

While working on a lathe, you may softly hum the Names but not too audibly.

Regarding friends asking you for spiritual help, Satsangis may offer solace and comfort—and that is not a negligible thing—but not spiritual help in the sense that you attempt to heal the sick by your power, for you have not yet developed that power and it would only scatter what little you have got. However, you may draw their attention to spiritual realities and spiritual comforts, and render whatever physical service is possible.

I appreciate your love and gratitude, and would ask you to utilize it in going within and meeting the Master there.

* * *

52.   When the concentration is complete, the Sound will come of itself. The function of the Sound is to pull the soul up. The Sound cannot pull it up unless the attention has been withdrawn from the entire body by means of Repetition, just as a magnet cannot attract a piece of iron which is lying beyond its magnetic field. It is the function of Simran (Repetition of the five Holy Names) to bring about the stillness and concentration of mind. Repetition should be performed while the attention is fixed at the eye centre. In other words, when performing Simran, please try to peep into the darkness which is visible to the closed eyes, but without any strain on the eyes. To begin with listening to the Sound, at the sacrifice of Simran, is putting the cart before the horse.

Our spiritual journey begins from the toes of the feet and

ends at the crown of the head. We come up to the eyes via Simran. From there we travel to the fifth stage, at the top of the head, with the help of the Sound Current. Therefore, we cannot start with the Sound Current so long as our attention is held in the lower portion of the body, below the eye centre.

This method is natural, though very slow. It requires years of practice to make the mind motionless, accustomed, as it has been for ages, to wander at will. Simran will act as a bridle in the mouth of an unbroken colt. Therefore, the time spent on Repetition should never be considered wasted.

You are quite right in saying that you cannot picture to yourself any object or person whom you have never seen. So you need not concentrate on the form of the Master but, instead, try to see the darkness within while performing Repetition.

No doubt this world is full of people who have no regard for the feelings of others. One feels miserable at the sight of strife and suffering around him. As you complete your concentration, you will also begin to rise above the circumstances that surround you. Again, I shall urge upon you to work hard on your Simran and not to expect results in a hurry. Slow and steady wins the race.

* * *

53. The foundation of the practice is the ability to withdraw the current of consciousness from the body and hold it at the eye centre, so that it may come in contact with Nam. This is naturally a slow process but, when achieved, the results are indeed remarkable.

Stilling the mind is achieved only by degrees, as the mind is in the habit of going out. Besides, the stored impressions of ages, in our subconscious mind begin to come to the surface when we begin our meditations. Simran (Repetition of the five Holy Names) is the only remedy. Repetition, in course of time, will solve all these difficulties and also take you to the eye centre. Please attend to your Simran regularly and devote as much time to it as you can.

* * *

54. I note your problems and your experiences. There is nothing like inner conviction. However, unless we have elevated our consciousness by Simran and concentrated it at the eye centre, this conviction and satisfaction may not be permanent; hence there may be questions and doubts.

One cannot ignore one's household and domestic duties, but one should accustom oneself to attend to them in a spirit of duty and yet find time for Spiritual Practices also. As you are able to devote yourself to Simran and meditation, you will find it easier to overcome these obstacles and will also find more pleasure in your meditations.

* * *

55. Your problem is both physical and mental. The first is easily dealt with, although the physical and mental act and react on each other. A good nourishing diet should replenish your energy and enable you to meet the situation, but to worry is no good. Worry never helped anybody and it never will.

If other people do not behave as they should, try to rise above the situation and do not mind them at all but go on doing your duty, and your mind will be at peace. Your attitude of having good and loving feelings towards others is quite correct and very helpful for, after all, things affect us only as we take them. One automatically reaps what he has sown and, if you sow kindness and good-will all around you, it is bound to return to you with interest.

Most of us seek the Truth, but it is not possible to find Truth outside. You must seek it within yourself and, when you have realized it within yourself, you will see it everywhere. You have been instructed in this Science and explained the technique of 'going in' and, after you practice the technique diligently, you will make spiritual progress and become indifferent to the squabbles of the world. Your progress is to be judged by the extent to which you have been able to vacate the body, *i.e.* to make it numb on account of the withdrawal of consciousness. This is the way to rise above the pettiness of the world and make spiritual progress.

* * *

56. As a rule, concentration becomes difficult when we have cares and worries, for then the attention sticks to the heart centre instead of rising up to the eye centre. We should take the right steps to meet the situation, so far as it lies in our power, and then worry no more. We should leave the rest to be worked out as the Master thinks fit.

When you sit for your meditation firmly banish all cares and anxieties for the time being at least and start the repetition of the five Names while holding the attention in the eye centre, with no other thought in your mind—not even the thought of going up or of measuring your progress. When you have done this for some time, it will enable you to concentrate on your work too.

It is the thought of what might possibly happen that preys upon the mind and makes you feel so distressed and depressed. Why should you think at all of going insane ? Why dwell upon such wrong, and harmful notions ? Surely there is nothing in the practices themselves to induce such a condition; rather, it is the reverse. Give as much time to meditation as you conveniently can and do not try to force results. Such a practice should result in happiness and strength.

"How to love the Master?" Repetition of the Names should be done diligently, at the proper centre, to the exclusion of all other thoughts. As you follow the Path with faith in and reliance on the Master, love will also develop. Faith in the Master while resigning ourself to His will and utilizing our faculties to the best of our knowledge, is one way of developing love.

There are no restrictions on Radha Soami disciples about marriage except that they must avoid over-indulgence, and not neglect their meditation.

* * *

57. The way of the spirit is so quick that you can get an answer in a few seconds when once the contact with the Inner Master has been established.

The view of worldly-minded people about the success and failure of life is utterly wrong and misleading. Their aims and objects are limited to the gains and pleasures of this world only. They do not understand the immense value of human life on this plane, nor its purpose and goal. We should pay no heed to their opinions. They do not realize that the sole object of human life here is to 'go in' and make contact with the Inner Master and the Sound Current, so as to get release from the cycle of births and deaths, to which we have been subjected ever since the world was made.

People do immense harm to themselves by failing to see that death will separate them from all that they love and that they may not get the opportunity of a human incarnation again for ages. Blessed are they who have learned this lesson, even through the failures of life, which are indeed better than worldly success if they teach us this lesson.

The primary object of sex is the propagation of the species. It is the law of nature, and there is nothing sinful in the proper use of this function by keeping the end in view. The secondary object is to make home-life bright with mutual love. Sex for enjoyment is indulgence, and indulgence should be avoided as it makes meditation and concentration difficult. Everything which hinders our spiritual progress is sinful. This is the distinction between virtue and vice—good and bad—according to the Masters. The real method of overcoming sexual desires is by concentrating our attention currents in the eye focus and connecting them with the Sound Current. This contact brings the sex impulse under control. This is the real and natural victory over sex.

Dreams occur when the attention descends from the eye centre down to the throat centre. The eye centre is the seat of full consciousness. If we go down, our consciousness goes on decreasing until we descend into the navel centre. Then we experience deep sleep and are utterly unconscious. Dreams are mostly the results of our day's thoughts and actions. Sometimes, in the case of disciples of the Masters, dreams are utilized by the Master to wash away karma. Those who have gained mastery in Sound practice, do not allow their soul to descend lower than the eye centre, even in sleep or rest. They take their soul to higher planes and remain wakeful within, even in sleep.

* * *

58.   Our spiritual journey begins from the feet and ends at the top of the head. It may be divided into two parts. The first is the withdrawal of the consciousness to the eye centre, thereby completing the concentration, which means the separation of the Vital Current from the physical body. This is done by the Repetition of the five Holy Names, which is the simplest and the surest method. The second part is the inner journey from the eye centre upward, and this is done by catching the Sound which is vibrating in all of us and leads to our Eternal Home.

The first part is a bit dry and tedious in the beginning, but becomes sweet and tasteful when one experiences the withdrawal of the current from the body.

* * *

59.   The best way to help others is to set an example of good and chaste conduct, and to work hard on concentration. When a soul is ready, the Master will Himself arrange for it to be taken into His fold. There is no need for direct propaganda. If you find somebody who is particularly interested, give him a few hints; otherwise, let others go their way and you go yours.

Yes, your view about the five Holy Names is quite correct. As the soul's path from the region of the Negative Power must necessarily take it through the regions ruled by the Negative

Power, the Masters have deemed it proper to indicate the Names of the rulers of those regions. These rulers are the guardians of the Path and place no obstructions in the way of those who carry out the repetition of Holy Names.

First, it is necessary to eradicate all worldly desires from the mind in order to make better progress in the spiritual journey, as desires lead to rebirth. Secondly, hard labour at Repetition, with attention fixed at the eye centre is necessary to bring about concentration of mind, which is the first real step toward Spiritual Progress.

* * *

60. I note your concern at your apparent lack of progress after a time——————— though at first, after Initiation, you had 'wonderful uplift'; also your inability to focalize your attention sufficiently at the eye centre. As you probably know, our attention has been 'out' for ages and to draw it 'in' again requires both time and effort. The tendencies established for such a long time are at once up against us when we attempt any reorientation. It is certainly not impossible, but it is naturally difficult and slow. For some it is slower and more difficult than it is for others.

The same applies to focussing the attention at the eye centre. Our consciousness permeates the entire body, down to our toes. We have to draw it up again and bring it to the eye centre, and send it upward. It is then that the door is opened. But the drawing up of consciousness or shaking it loose from the material body is a slow and laborious process. It has been called "the way of the ant", which first laboriously picks up grains of sugar from amongst the grains of sand with which it is mixed, then slowly moves up the wall, very frequently slipping down and then laboriously moving up again.

All that is required is to persist with patience, hope and faith. Then success will one day be yours. Leave the rest to the Master and remember that effort is never wasted.

* * *

61.   I am glad to know that your health has improved by abstinence from animal food and intoxicating drinks. The visions which you have described are due to concentration of the mind and the purity of soul. But they cannot be called voluntary in the sense that you could command them at will. They were the result of accidental concentration, brought about by external circumstances beyond your control. Radha Soami prescribes a method of practice by which concentration can be brought about 'at will'. If you want to get the method, you should contact a true Master.

* * *

62.   Glad to know that you have received Initiation and are trying to practise concentration. You should try to focus your attention in the eye centre, between the two eyebrows. As concentration develops, your soul will have vision of the inner solar system and, after crossing it, you may expect to see the astral form of the Master.

I wish that the Master may grant you more spare time for carrying on your spiritual practice every day. In this world everyone of us is bound by past karma, which must be undergone. Every human life has some good and some bad karma, although the proportions of each are not always the same. So every one of us has to pass through some good and some bad times. The same is the case with yourself and your children.

Spiritual progress makes one indifferent to worldly surroundings and enables one to rise above adverse circumstances. That is the only way. While alive, an Initiate is to vacate the body in the same way people do at death, but at will, and see what lies beyond. The attention has to be withdrawn from the body and concentrated at the eye centre. This is slow process and is connected with past karma. It is a life-long process.

* * *

63. Am pleased to note that you are trying to focus your attention at the eye centre, which is the first important step. However, this requires time and perseverance. As you yourself feel, sometimes in the beginning one feels very much elated and filled with a sense of power. Sometimes the attention slips out or down and one has to put in no small effort to bring it back again. Yet this has to be done. At last the attention will be firmly fixed there. Skill and expertise in any branch of human effort depend on constant practice. The control of the mind is not easy. It has been out from the eye centre for ages and will not lose its outward tendencies easily.

The pain in the legs and the lower part of the body is due to the withdrawal of consciousness. It will not last long but it is unavoidable in the beginning. If you find it unbearable, you may slow the pace. Also do not get up from Bhajan at once, but gradually, after stroking the legs.

Consciousness is spread through the entire body, right down to the toes, and is very intimately associated with the body. The separation of this long and intimate association is naturally painful, but with practice it becomes easy and natural. Then you will pass through the portals of death and the gates of light, into Spiritual Regions. It is easier to bear this pain now, and by degrees, than to bear it in all its entirety at the time of death; for when the consciousness begins to separate from the physical body, pain is inevitable.

Please do not fear nor worry about any faces, however miserable or ill-looking, that you may see; but go on repeating the Names with love and confidence, and remember that the protecting Power of the Master is always with you. The horrible sights are due to old, may be age-long associations and affinities, but are powerless to exercise any evil influence as long as you take your stand in Nam. They will disappear of themselves.

* * *

64. There should be no strain or effort to see or hear anything. As concentration improves and the consciousness is drawn up, the Sound will automatically become stronger. In the beginning the emphasis should be on vacating the body.

I appreciate your sentiments but the real feet of the Master are within you and it should be the aim and ambition of every disciple to reach up to the feet of the Master within. Love and devotion are of great help in realizing this ambition, and the more you devote yourself to meditation and begin to go in, the more will your love increase.

* * *

65. The important thing is to withdraw your attention from outward objects and turn it within. The feeling of exhilaration is a sign of concentration, but the body need not and should not be in motion. All thought and energy should be directed towards the eye centre. Please pay no attention to the body, and if there is a movement, discourage it.

You are very fortunate that you have glimpses of the Master. As you learn to hold the attention more steadily, you will be able to see the Master within more clearly and in greater detail.

* * *

66. Yes, it is right that everybody is not evolved enough to tread the Path of the Masters. But this should not preclude anyone from making a beginning.

Regarding using one's will-power to curb one's desires, there are two ways of killing desire and attaining desirelessness: One that is generally followed by common folk is to fulfil the desire and get satiated. The other is to create in the mind indifference to desire by means of reasoning and self-control. Self-control would require an effort of one's will-power. The mind is like a restive colt and loves to go where it is forbidden to go. Like a colt, it should be restrained by degrees and not all at once; otherwise it will break the restraining chains and fly in the prohibited direction with force.

The Masters say that one should give up all animal food and alcoholic drinks before one is fit to tread the Path which leads to the control of mind and desirelessness. Therefore, besides reading the literature, you should try to give up the prohibited diet and see if you can eschew it throughout the remainder of your life without any bad effect on your health. Then write to me again after acquiring a confirmed habit of a vegetarian and a teetotaller. When it is necessary, the cooking of meat for others is not prohibited, but it is not desirable. However, one should not eat it himself under any circumstances.

* * *

67. You should not think of breathing or paying any heed to it while you are doing your Simran, just as you do not think of breathing when you are reading a book. Breathing goes on automatically and requires no attention.

* * *

68. Apart from the question of taking life, eggs— whether fertile or infertile—are an exciting food, and for persons who engage in spiritual work, non-exciting food is necessary. Our mind is affected by what we eat, and the food we eat, conditions the mind. There is a proverb in India to the effect that our mind is according to what we eat. Fertile and infertile eggs should both be avoided.

* * *

69. It is, no doubt, a slow and laborious process especially in the beginning, but with steadiness and perseverance the goal is achieved, even as you slowly and steadily have improved your health. When you do your Simran intensively, with love and faith, it becomes automatic "like the spinning of a wheel", as you have put it. This is the result of your past karmas.

You may arrange your affairs and household in such a way as to give you convenience and ease in doing your spiritual duty. Then turn to Simran while concentrating the attention at the eye centre. When you have been able to vacate the body, the disturbing element would be removed and you will be able to get full advantage from the Sound Current. The test of complete concentration is that you should have no consciousness of the body and should be superconscious within.

There is this important difference: In dream we are at the throat centre, but in Bhajan we vacate the body by concentration at the eye centre. Love, faith and perseverance are the keys to success.

* * *

70. As you know, meditation is entirely mental process, and postures in traditional yoga positions are only aids and not absolutely necessary prerequisites. If bodily infirmity or weakness constantly draws the attention to the lower limbs, it is decidedly better to adopt an easier position and to keep the attention concentrated at the eye centre.

———— but the aim should always be to increase these periods gradually so that you can ultimately sit for two and a half hours at a stretch. There should be no hurry in doing so. Rather, the progress should be consolidated.

Pronunciation of these Words does not always come easy to western people. By and by you will be able to do so, and there will be no difficulty.

* * *

71. I am very pleased to read your letter——and your appreciation of the Great Master. He truly had infinite patience. Even now He helps and supervises the destinies of His flock.

The vision of the Dear Master is always pacifying and blissful, and drives 'the five' out. As your mind learns to remain concentrated at the eye centre, this vision may be had at will. However, you should not stop here but go on still further so that you may always swim in His love and peace.

* * *

72. The Master never dies. He is Energy, He is Sound Current and He is always watching over you. You should continue your meditation with love and faith. So long as your attention does not go in and contact the inner Master so as to receive His instructions, you may refer your difficulties to me. You should regularly give time to meditation, try to vacate the body and hear the Sound.

* * *

73. Things in themselves do not really matter so much as our reaction to them. Our own mind is our worst enemy but when it is properly and firmly handled, and correctly disciplined, it can also be our best friend and helper. An optimistic attitude is very helpful, but what really and substantially helps us is Simran (the Repetition of the five Holy Names). It is a wonderful talisman, the significance and efficacy of which you will realize only when you devote sufficient time (two and one-half to three hours daily) to it, to the exclusion of all other thoughts and cares. Incidentally, it will help you in withdrawing your consciousness from the lower parts of the body to the proper centre, after which real spiritual progress begins.

The hazy atmosphere of bliss should change into more definite and blissful experiences based on Light and Sound. The Sound Current, of course, pervades all your being but it must help you to go up, pull you up in fact. This will happen only when you loosen your lower attachments, rule out harmful or inadmissible desires and surrender yourself to Nam or Word.

This is possible only with an intensive course of Simran, and this is also the best and the most practical way of showing your gratefulness to the Great Master from Whom you received so much Grace.

* * *

74.   I appreciate your problem. It is characteristic of the mind that all sorts of questions and problems will force themselves on your attention at the time of Simran. Dismiss all irrelevant thoughts with an effort of the will. Every time you do that and assert your will, you make your path comparatively easier, even though your success may not be apparent to you.

Simran is the foundation, and the foundation must be strong. It is helpful, very helpful, not only in your Spiritual efforts but also in the worldly sphere. There is hardly any limit to what can be achieved by proper and intensive Simran, *i.e.* regular and one-pointed Simran, to the exclusion of all other thoughts. You may do the Simran during day time or any other time that suits you, if you find the early morning hours inconvenient.

* * *

75.   Your progress in meditation is quite satisfactory, and as you persevere you will have still better concentration. The numbness of the lower limbs and a feeling of lightness throughout the body are signs of concentration.

* * *

76.   The Radha Soami Faith does not impose dogmatic beliefs. It teaches the successful method used by all the Saints in their achievement of God-realization, as a result of their research. Each one is required to find out for himself the Truths discovered by the Masters, after 'going in' and ascending to higher regions. You will admit that unless we have faith in the method revealed by the Master, we cannot expect to make progress. Faith in the Master's instructions is necessary for advancement on the Path. If a student has no faith in his teacher, he will not learn.

Karma is washed away by the practice of Sound Current and, as the soul goes up, the will power continues to grow stronger. The karma is cancelled by hearing the Sound Current within.

Man is the top of creation and if his deeds are those of a man, he will continue to advance. However, if he stoops to low actions like those of animals, birds or insects, he is bound to become what he made himself while in the form of man.

* * *

77. You say that you feel a desire to follow the spiritual teachings of the Radha Soami Faith but find difficulty in following the vegetarian diet.

God has fashioned the human body in such a masterly way that all the eye can see in the outside world has been placed inside the human body. The Microcosm contains the Macrocosm, and the Creator has seated Himself within the human body. You can have a full and clear view of the Macrocosm and all that it contains by gaining access into the human body, at the eye centre. Christ says "The Kingdom of God is within you." It is nowhere to be found in the outside world. By studying oneself, one can study the universe. The whole 'Secret' will be found in the portion of the human body which is above the eyes. But that 'Spiritual Structure' is behind the curtain of the mind, in the deep recesses of the mind, and our mind has been wandering outside for thousands of lives.

It is to man alone that the privilege has been vouchsafed to withdraw his attention from the outside world and, by thus taking his attention within himself, to study the inner worlds and their machinery. So the first and foremost duty of man is to take his attention back, within himself, to the place whence it had come out. That place is called the 'Third Eye' or the

'Centre of Consciousness'. It is to that place that the Current of Consciousness flows down from above. 'Sound' emanates from it; hence Christ called it 'WORD', and Dr. Johnson, in his book, has referred to it as the Audible Life Stream. This is the straight road that takes us back to our True Spiritual Home, in the top of the head, whence the soul originally descended into the body. In other words, our Spiritual Journey starts from the toes of our feet and finishes at the top of our head.

As our consciousness withdraws from the extremities of the body up to the eye centre, or as the Spiritual Current becomes separated from the matter that envelops and conceals it, our frailties and weaknesses begin to disappear. Lust, anger and other negative sister passions leave, and positive powers are awakened in us. It is then that man realizes his real value and true worth.

In order to undertake this journey, it is essential that one should abstain from animal food (meat, fish, eggs and anything containing them) and alcoholic drinks. These articles have a tendency to scatter one's attention. Thus they hinder concentration. They add considerably to the already too heavy debt of karmas, which should be reduced as much as possible. So, one who desires to tread the Path of Spirituality must give up those articles that are a hindrance in the Way. I have great regard and sympathy for you, but you will kindly realize that it is not possible to relax this condition because, so long as one does not give up the animal diet, one cannot begin the Spiritual Journey.

* * *

78. There are numerous hidden powers dormant within the human body, which can be awakened and mastered gradually, with effort. When we send a child to school, the school master does not impart anything to the child from the outside; he merely awakens the child's dormant faculties in his brain. This is done gradually, through daily exercises. The same is the case with spiritual faculties. The positive proof of such faculties can be had when one looks within himself.

The human body is a laboratory for spiritual research, and proof can be had by taking the attention currents inside. If you can complete your concentration, that is, if you can collect the attention currents (which are permeating the entire body) in the eye focus and can invert your gaze (which means seeing inside rather than outside), you will find that there is intense light within you as are also numberless planes where unceasing music is going on.

If a human being can take his attention inward, probe inside, and take possession of the wealth which the Almighty Lord has put there, then the five foes can be conquered. The Sound Current or Audible Life Stream is inside and can be heard by anyone who turns his attention inward. If man inverts his hearing faculties, he can hear it. This is a highly technical process and cannot be explained adequately in books. It can be obtained by personal contact with a living Master. At first, one should try to complete his concentration, for which there are various methods. When the attention has gone in, one meets with prophets and sages at different planes, even though they died long, long ago.

* * *

79. As for concert and symphonic music, it is all right. However, the outer music does not feed the soul, but only the mind. It is not taboo, but it should not be a hindrance in Bhajan and should not distract your attention at the time of Bhajan. This is the acid test. We ought to try to 'go in', and anything which prevents that or drags us out is harmful. Of course it is different in the case of different individuals. Our aim should be to develop and be one with the Heavenly Music within.

* * *

80. The answers to some of the questions which you have asked can best be grasped after you have made some progress in Bhajan. As far as possible, all efforts should be directed towards 'going in'.

Each soul is like a drop from that great Ocean of Consciousness. By His 'Mauj' (Will or Pleasure of the Lord) souls come down and develop and degenerate into separate individual entities by contact with mind and matter. Then, after contacting a Master and by following His instructions, they realize their Spiritual heritage, work their way up according to His directions and return to their Original Home whence they had come and, in time, get merged again into that Ocean.

The past karmas as well as the grace of the Lord are the determining factors which bring any individual to the Master.

Spirit is all-pervading and when the coverings of mind and matter are removed it merges in the Word. The Masters say that every plant, every tree and every grain has soul in it. The difference in the degree of consciousness in plant life and in animal life is due to the fact that in this physical plane the soul is under the sway of the mind which, in the lower creation, is not fully conscious on account of deficiency in the five tattwas. All souls are alike. Soul is life, soul is light or consciousness which is clouded by mind and matter, and darkness does not comprehend it. In the lower forms of creation, the darkness increases and consciousness decreases.

It is not quite correct to say that the Masters did not appear in the three preceding Yugas. In his books, Kabir Sahib states that he appeared in every Yuga, but few people accepted his teachings. In Kaliyuga, the number of people who are ready and prepared to try the method of the Masters has increased to a vast extent, as people are weary of the short-lived pleasures of the world. The soul remains within the cycle of births and deaths until contact is made with a True Master.

It is true that the real teaching of Christ is the 'WORD' or the 'SOUND CURRENT', and the Sermon on the Mount represents only the ethical teachings.——Do not discuss the doctrine too much but draw attention to "the Word that was with God", and which is God still, and which can be contacted by proper means. It is wrong for anyone to think that Sant Mat inculcates selfish personal salvation.

* * *

81. 'Sohang' means 'I am He', but it does not refer to the individual as he is here and now confined in the body and the mind. It refers to a definite stage in the spiritual progress of the individual and is not to be confused with the assertion of those who even in the present imperfect and bound state of the individual, claim identity with Brahm.

Let me explain more clearly: We have first of all to concentrate at the eye centre, between the two eyebrows, and repeat the five Holy Names at least two hours every day, if not more. Thus we withdraw our consciousness, which now pervades the entire body, up to the eye centre. Here, at this centre, we contact the region which is ruled by Jot Niranjan, catch the next higher Shabd and reach Trikuti or the Mental Region, *i.e.* the region of Karan or Causal Mind. From this region we pass on to the Third Stage where the soul is free from the three covers—physical, astral and causal—and, being rid of those dragging chains is strongly impelled onwards and reaches the Fourth Region or the Stage called 'Sohang' in Sant Mat, and to which you have referred. Having shed these covers and realized its spiritual nature and its kinship with the Lord, the soul joyfully exclaims: 'I am He!' because it realizes that the two are of the same essence—one is the Ocean and the other is a drop from that Ocean. You will thus see that it involves no contradiction in any way.

The Five Names are the Names of the Lords or Rulers of the vast Spiritual Regions which the soul has to cross before reaching Sach Khand. Simran or Repetition of these Names, as directed, brings in concentration. But it is Shabd which will draw you up and take you from one region to another, right up to Sach Khand.

You can hear the Shabd now, in your present state of progress. However, at this stage the Shabd will not be able to draw you up because the attention is still tied in the body.

I hope this explains your question.

* * *

82. Time changes and will go on changing, but Nam does not change. The current of Nam goes on as usual. It is Nam which changes the times and brings about all changes. Till we are able to put our consciousness in Nam, we will be subject to changes, now happy and now miserable. That is why the Saints repeatedly exhort us to withdraw our conscious attention from the nine doors of the body and fix it in Shabd. As we do this and our attention is withdrawn from the body and enjoys the bliss of Nam, we develop power of endurance and spiritual depth. After crossing the perishable states of Maya, we enter the eternal state of Nam and, freed from the cycle of births and deaths, are entitled to everlasting happiness.

From the day the Satguru initiates a person, He internally contrives in such a way that while the person undergoes his Pralabdh or Fate Karma, arrangements for his reaching Sach Khand also go on side by side. If the disciple works with love and faith in the words of the Satguru, and carries out His instructions diligently and faithfully, he will attain peace and calm. On the other hand, if the disciple is negligent in carrying out the orders, he is rocked by pleasure and pain at different times, and only when he is unhappy, does he think of the Satguru. This also is for the disciple's good.

The Satguru makes no mistakes. He is Shabd. He is the Lord in human form. Till one vacates the nine doors of the body and realizes the Satguru within, his Dhyan (contemplation) is imperfect and his faith in the Satguru is also not steady.

Does a mother ever wish to see her child unhappy ? But when it is ill, she gets the medicine from the doctor and gives it to the child, unmindful of its cries and protests. She has at heart the good of the child.

Do not feel frustrated. Just try to have a peep within. the Satguru is with you and His love suffers no change.

* * *

83. Sound, stars and light are all inside. When our mind ascends, it hears the Sound and sees the Light. But when our mind is disturbed, it falls down and cannot listen and hear. Therefore, unless and until our concentration is perfect, *i.e.* until the mind and the soul—after vacating the entire body— collect in the eye centre, the internal Sound cannot be heard clearly and continuously, and no progress can be made on the Path.

It is not an easy matter to take the currents of the mind and the soul out of the body. It is a very slow process and requires hard labour for years. Until one has completed his concentration and until one has gathered together the mind currents at some centre inside, it is a mistake even to think of rendering practical aid to others. No doubt it is a good idea to give spiritual help to others but before that can be done, it is necessary that one should have personal experience. It is not sufficient merely to hear sounds and see lights.

The Western mind is apt to expect quick results. However, it is not the work of months or even a year or two to be able to train the mind which has been accustomed to wander outwards for numerous births in the past. So long as the mind does not turn back and sit still in the 'Third Eye', an individual cannot be said to have stood on his own legs and neither can he help others to any appreciable degree.

* * *

84. You do well to keep the Master in your thoughts and in your mind. That is our only solace in this wicked world. The Negative Power, which governs our world and the regions up to Brahm, is a cruel magistrate who punishes us for our past deeds whether we know their nature or not. It is karmic debt which he must exact without any idea that the punishment should be for reforming the one who is being punished. Yet our conscience often warns us against an evil deed. This conscience may be born of the results and sufferings of past bad karmas. The world could not go on if the memory of past births were not effaced completely.

Let not the evil and selfishness of the world depress your heart. Remain cheerful in the thought of the love and protection of the Master.

* * *

85. Before you begin your meditation, please perform Dhyan of the Master for fifteen minutes. Then, when you begin Repetition, if any star or the Master's form is visible inside, continue to look at it. If you see nothing inside, then continue to look into the darkness while repeating the Names.

* * *

86. Regarding your statement that man is a lonely traveller in the journey of life, by and by, as you vacate the body from below, give up the path of the mind and travel the path of Nam, you will feel that you are not quite alone and that the Master always is your companion.

You say that you are very much afraid of death. As your attention goes in and leaves the body, the fear of death will become less and less.

As to your difficulty in overcoming attachment to worldly things, that will also go gradually, in the same proportion as your attention goes in. He who has separated himself from his body, has separated himself from the world and this is the real renunciation.

You complain that your mind keeps wandering during meditation. Watch over the mind. If the mind sees anything inside, whether it is the form of the Master or only darkness, then go on gazing steadily at it, all the while repeating the five Holy Names. The mind will become still. However, when you fail to fix your attention while repeating the Holy Names, the mind will wander because the peculiarity of the mind is that it shall not remain idle.

* * *

87.   No, you are not permitted even to whisper the five Holy Names in the ear of your aged mother who is ill and who is not a Satsangi. Show her the photograph of Master Sawan Singh Ji.

* * *

88.   When you sit for Repetition, you should try to keep the body in one posture for two hours and while repeating the five Holy Names, fix your attention in the eye centre. Take care that your mind does not do anything else. If you continue this for some time then, by degrees, the currents of the mind and the soul will leave the lower extremities of the body and will begin to collect in the eye centre. Your legs and arms will feel benumbed. When this happens, you should be satisfied that your Repetition is going on all right. Please do not change your posture so long as you sit. Keep watch over your mind and do not allow it to generate any thought. It should occupy itself only with Repetition at that time. Thus, as your attention slowly withdraws, you will become unconscious of the body. You will be conscious within, and your mind will be repeating the five Names. Even if one were to sit in one posture for two hours, without repetition, his legs would begin to feel numb. When you have completed your time of Repetition, then sit on your feet, in the prescribed posture, and hear the sound for half an hour. Listen to whatever Sound you can get.

* * *

89.   Several kinds of scenes and visions appear when the door begins to open. The result is that the devotee gives up Repetition and engages himself in seeing those visions or scenes. This is a mistake. When scenes and visions appear, one should not give up Repetition nor his seat in the eye centre. It is only then that withdrawal will be complete and that one will be fit to sit inside.

* * *

90.   There are two paths: The path of the mind and the path of Nam. In the path of the mind, the soul descends below the eye centre and is entangled in the world through the mind and the senses. The path of Nam is the ascent of the soul to regions above the eye centre, after divesting itself from the mind and the senses, collecting all its energy in the eye centre and contacting the Sound Current.

* * *

91.   I am pleased to find that you are making very satisfactory progress. It is due in no small measure to your past karma, and the attitude which you have adopted. This is the correct attitude in matters spiritual and it induces humility and curbs the mind.

The experiences which you have described are not abnormal and represent the struggle between matter and consciousness. As you draw up the soul from the lower parts of the body to the seat of consciousness, there is sometimes a wrench. Happily it is over and you can expect to go on smoothly on your upward journey. The numbness of the body is the natural result of concentration and drawing up of consciousness, and you should count yourself fortunate in achieving such satisfactory progress within a very short time. The upward pull also is a mark of quick concentration and when it is complete you will see the light within and the Sound also will become clearer and finer.

The Sound which you have been hearing for so many years has a spiritual background and has nothing to do with any physical disorder. Hence the doctors were helpless.

* * *

92. The gradually increasing numbness of the body is the acid test and a proof of the withdrawal of the consciousness, and so far it was very satisfactory. What you call spinal manipulation or spinal correction within during Meditation is not Sant Mat and can be looked upon as an aberration influenced by 'Sanskaras' or dormant tendencies of a past birth when practising a crude form of yoga. The rhythmic swinging of the body during meditation is also due to a partial sub-conscious acceptance of the past tendencies. I am glad you at last resisted it, and that is the proper attitude.

Once you are firm and realize that the only correct, natural and proper way for you is to withdraw your consciousness and concentrate it at the eye centre by means of *Simran i.e.* Repetition of the five Holy Names, without any manipulation during the sitting, this will cease and you will enjoy your Bhajan again as before. Please remove all fear and dread, and discard altogether the idea of entity control. . . was no doubt right in discounting any such idea. For health you may follow the doctor's advice and take medicines or injections.

Please do not harbour any fear or weakness but be firm and steadfast in the strength and protecting power of the Master. Please go on with your Bhajan in the same manner as before and with the same confidence, and resist any movement of the head or any manipulation whatsoever when sitting for spiritual practice. I shall always be glad to hear from you.

Your inner experience is right; inner scenes and lights vary according to the rise and fall of attention.

* * *

93. I have gone through your long letter and am really glad to learn that you have got rid of those manipulations and no longer feel them during your spiritual practice. You had to suffer so much pain and mental disquiet. However, all's well that ends well. The occasional jerk that you experience now and then will also disappear. It should be ignored. It is a pity that your advisers were ill-informed. Anyway, you can always write here for information on any doubtful point.

As for the feeling and pulsations in the forehead, it is all right. Only you should not try to force things but you should do your repetition calmly and gently. Nor should you worry about finding the exact eye centre. It would only distract your attention. When the concentration is complete, the eye centre will be located automatically. The soul will find its own way. There is no reason for disappointment. Slow and steady wins the race. The numbness will be more complete and by practice will also last longer.

You are doing well and there is no reason for you to feel disappointed or dissatisfied. The early morning hours are certainly very good and the late evening hours too may be utilized if they suit you, but do not reduce your food and sleep to such an extent that the body gets weak and you find it difficult to perform normal duties. Nor should you deny rest to the body. But as the concentration becomes complete or nearly so and you get into the habit of gradually increasing the period of concentration, sleep will be reduced without any conscious effort on your part. When the attention goes naturally to the eye centre that is without being forced, there is neither sleepiness nor fatigue.

I appreciate your love and devotion; and they are responsible for the experiences you have narrated and the protection you have received. Yes, all these experiences are correct and you should regard yourself as very fortunate in having them.

The experience you had during the so-called five Bhajanless days, that is, brilliant white light surrounded by twinkling lights, was real and correct and was due to your attention being subconsciously at the eye centre. It was perfectly natural for the attention to be riveted on the central white light as also the suction. The nearer you draw to this light, the greater will be the suction, for you have to pierce and cross it. You did miss something there, for you should not have battled against this suction. You should have remained relaxed and allowed yourself to be drawn up, mentally repeating the Names all the while. Love and faith are the keynotes.

P.S. Subconscious repetition of Names may be continued all the day, as suggested, provided it does not interfere with your work. Generally it does not; *but there should be no repetition while listening to* the Sound. At that time *all the attention* should be in the Sound.

The top of the head is the place whence the Sound emanates. We hear it in the ear only because we are accustomed to hear sounds through the ears.

* * *

94. The first thing I have to say is that the body should be afforded rest when it needs rest and there should be no attempt to force things or to put unnecessary strain anywhere. Whatever is achieved gradually, is lasting.

The work of withdrawing the consciousness from the lower centre on which it has been dwelling for thousands of years is not a very easy job and cannot be done over night; though, of course, love and faith are wonderful accelerators.

The heaviness and forehead sensations are due to unnecessary strain, and strain at a time when the system needed rest. Please do not try to read on such occasions but just lie down and relax, and if you are inclined to repeat the Names, do it gently, without forcing the attention up. Do not deny yourself rest. . . . Your last experience was during this off period.

Yes, you are right in accepting the natural and correct pace. It is a labour of years but there is no reason either for despair or impatience. Let things happen as they do naturally. You cannot hustle the power within.

* * *

95. It is satisfactory to learn that your eyes do not feel tired now and you feel that you are more accurately near the eye focus. You need not try to find the focus, for this results in some strain. As the consciousness is drawn up and the concentration becomes complete, it will automatically find the eyefocus.

It is good to rest and relax but rest should be mental and not only physical. The mind, in spite of yourself, goes back to the same subject and hence the recrudescence of the trouble. Relaxation is not complete and the mind and nerves easily go back to familiar paths.

Nor should you subject your eyes to strain in any way. Every organ should be used only to the extent to which it can be used in a wholesome way. You may read now and then, but lightly, and do not risk any strain. Sewing, etc. is more or less a mechanical work and does not involve any participation of the mind. The strain comes where the mind is involved. Also, please do not analyze the situation too much. It keeps the picture constantly before the mind and stands in the way of complete relaxation.

There is no objection to students of R.S. associating with students travelling other spiritual paths but no secrets should be given out. . . . Yes, it is not blood pressure and there is no use consulting the doctor about it.

I am glad to hear of your progress and you need not feel the slightest hesitation in writing to me. Write as often as you like and long or short letters, as you please. The numbness of the body is a very good and encouraging sign, specially up to the shoulders. By and by it will be complete. It involves some bodily pain, which should be borne, but be gradual and do only as much as can be tolerated easily.

* * *

96.   I am gratified to note that you have adopted the right attitude. Our past karmas are translated into present inclinations, tendencies and mental attitudes. Our loves and hates, likes and dislikes have their roots in the distant past; but having realized this, we should act in such a way as to rise above them and to free ourselves from their shackles. The right course is to do your duty in a dispassionate spirit and leave the results to the Master.

You know more than your husband does, as he has not the benefits of the Sant Mat teachings and therefore you are expected to be more tolerant. You do well in recognizing your mistakes and avoiding them in the future. Yes, try your level best to undo the wrong and avoid mistakes in the future, even though your husband continues to feel angry and refers to them every now and then, for that is also a way to face and work off your karmas. And last but not least, give as much time to meditation and Sound practice as possible and remember that the Master watches the lives and actions of his loving disciples. Please also remember that argument and reason are not everything. Sentiment also is an important factor in this world and especially in the family. Give up argument and discussion, and things will become easier.

Your husband, whenever he is worried about financial difficulties, not being a Satsangi and unaware of the laws of karma, attributes them all to you and becomes unpleasant, but you know better. Whenever you feel dejected or sad as a result of such unpleasantness, turn in and try to repeat the Names or contact the Sound. When we are disgusted with the world, we may find it more easy to turn the mind inwards and obtain solace there.

* * *

97.   My dear and revered Satsangis . . . . nurtured and blessed by our beloved Satguru. During the illuminating discourses of Shri Huzur Sawan Singh Maharaj Ji, you must have heard a number of times :

> "I am the lowliest of all. Save me, all others are good. He is a friend of mine who in this realization liveth."
>
> *–Kabir*

Therefore brethren, if there is any sinner, worthless and guilty, it is I. Why? Because according to the Bani,

> "One should die before one's beloved.
> Despicable is life and all the world if one lives thereafter."

Huzur, however, teaches us that, in Sant Mat, greatness lies in surrender to the Will of the Master. I am powerless by myself to carry out His commands, and it is His benign grace alone that enables me to do His bidding.

Further, as to your inquiries about Nam, what shall I say save repeat to you the words of Huzur Maharaj Ji, who on reference being made to Him that until one had attained Par Brahm, one should not grant Initiation, had replied, "The real Nam should be dispensed only by one who has reached Sach Khand and that too with Master's explicit permission. Without this, the bearing of karmic burden of the initiate is no easy task. I also entrust to the care of Maharaj Ji (Baba Jaimal Singh), whomsoever I initiate." Now, when this Param Sant (Great

Saint) has thus enjoined, the disciples and devotees can draw their own inferences. I did not grant Initiation for nine months, though Huzur Maharaj Ji Himself, while in this mortal frame, bade me do so, and even left the command in writing. The reason for this had better be left unexplained.

This Dera belongs to our Gracious Satguru and is our Holiest Shrine. Huzur Baba Ji Maharaj and Huzur Sawan Singh Maharaj Ji have sanctified this place with 60 to 65 years of meditation and bestowal of the gift of Nam to seekers. Whatever service of the Sangat Huzur Sawan Singh Maharaj Ji has entrusted to me, I shall carry out with His Grace and Sustenance as long as He Wills; and, when He shall call me, I shall depart.

"At His behest I came; When He beckons I shall leave."
                                                    —*Guru Nanak*

There is nothing to be perturbed about. The Satguru, who rescued us from the raging fire of Pakistan and sacrificed His own life to atone for our sins, is every moment watching over and protecting us.

"Transcending the cycle of births and deaths, came our Redeemer. He gave us the gift of Nam and Bhakti, and merged us with the Lord Sublime."

Do not miss Bhajan and Simran. You have already witnessed the catastrophic happenings in the world around; and as for the future, who knows ? The only wealth that can accompany us is our Bhajan and Simran. Even the body we nurture night and day will have to be left behind. Nothing here is ours. Only two things belong to us—Satguru and Nam, but for these two things we have little love. Whether the mind likes it or not, you must give full time to spiritual practice regularly and without fail. At the time of meditation, try and make your mind motionless and hold the form of the Master in your eye centre. Gradually, the mind will give way and become still. This is not a day's job—it calls for the labour of years.

PART IV

A Spiritual Bouquet

[Points selected from
Sardar Bahadur Maharaj Jagat Singh's
private and public talks]

A Spiritual Bouquet

1. One does not become a Satsangi simply by being initiated. One must mould his life in accordance with the principles of Satsang. Every thought, speech and action must conform to them. Actions speak louder than words. Thoughts are even more potent. A Satsangi's daily conduct must bear the hall-mark of excellence and must reveal that he is the follower of a True Master.

* * *

2. An ounce of practice is better than a ton of knowledge. What use is it to know the principles if one does not live them. A learned person without practice is no better than a beast of burden carrying a load of books on its back. It is infinitely better to practise than to preach.

Example is better than precept. Ravana, the king of Lanka, was not only a learned scholar but was also the best commentator on the Vedas. His actions, however, belied his great erudition, for he stooped down to kidnapping the wife of another and suffered the decimation of his entire race as a consequence.

* * *

3. A pure heart is most essential for spiritual progress. You cannot expect a king to enter a filthy cabin. Even a dog does not sit in an unclean place. How can you expect God to enter a heart that is full of the passions of lust, anger, greed, attachment and pride or egotism ?

* * *

4. Our body is the temple of the living God. It must not be polluted with the intake of meat, eggs, alcoholic drinks, etc. Nor must falsehood, lust, anger, avarice, hatred, pride, vanity, egotism and worldly attachments be allowed to have their sway. They must be swept clear to make it fit for His residence.

* * *

5. Never hurt the feelings of anyone. This is a sin which even God Himself does not pardon, because it cuts at the very root of spirituality. We should not thrust our views on others. An attitude of humility should be adopted and we should always speak kindly. Sheikh Farid, the great Muslim Mystic says :

> Farid! If thou longest to see the Beloved,
> Never hurt the feelings of any man.
> If people give thee fist blows,
> Do not thou beat them in return.
> Rather kiss their feet
> And take thou thy way Home.

* * *

6. Our inward Path is infested with robbers, but the worst is the opposite sex. This 'Chetan Maya' cheats by becoming sweet. Beware of this great danger. When the thought of the opposite sex comes into the mind, immediately stand 'at attention' like a soldier. You do this by drawing your attention instantly to the eye focus and concealing yourself behind the Master's Form. Shut yourself in that cabin. This is taking the attitude of standing 'at attention' in the spiritual way. Face the mind with courage and steadfastness. Do not lay down your arms before it. You never can win by prostrating yourself before an enemy. Give the mind a good slap in the face.

* * *

7. Cowards never conquer. Sant Mat is the Path of the valiant. They come into the field of battle with their 'head on their palms', as an offering to the Beloved Lord. No sacrifice is too great to win the Fort (the Palace of the Beloved).

Sohni loved Mahiwal, who lived by a river. She used to swim across on an earthen vessel to meet him. Once the vessel was replaced by an unbaked one and the river was in spate. She knew well that crossing would mean certain death, but she did not retrace her footsteps. She smilingly laid down her life at the altar of love. In our love for the Lord, we should emulate this dauntless woman. Be steadfast in your meditation. Persevere with it and do *not* give up as soon as there is the slightest pain in the limbs. This latter is, in fact, a sign of withdrawal of the soul current from the (tomb of) body which you so much adorn.

* * *

8. If you wish to tread the Path of the Master, be prepared to surrender your body, mind and possessions. Still your desires, give up attachment and be prepared to suffer taunts and ridicules. If you cannot bring yourself up to these ideals, you can hardly expect to succeed. Remember! you do not and cannot get anything in the world without having to pay the full price for it. It is only a fool who tries to get something for nothing. Even a person who imagines he has succeeded, has actually run into a new debt. So long as he owes even a farthing on this planet, he must return to make the payment. Not even a single grain that inadvertently enters your granary from a neighbour's field can go unaccounted. You simply must pay for what you get. The law is inviolable and it cannot be set aside. The payment may be either in kind or in coin or by transfer of an equivalent good karma, but payment there must be.

There is no gain without pain. The price of pleasure is pain. Gold you must dig out of a mine and for pearls you dive into a deep sea. No child is born without labour. What sacrifices does a man not make to achieve his objects of love ? Then how do you expect to realize the Lord without paying the proper price for it? You have to work hard and incessantly. You have to eat less, speak less and sleep less. You have virtually to shun society and glamour. You have to humble your mind and you must control your senses. All other desires must vanish and only the desire for God-realization must remain. There is no room for two in this narrow lane. There is place only for one, either God or Mammon. If you want to realize Him, you have to give up everything else. If you cannot do this, then simply give up the pursuit. Do not talk any more of the Lord or of His love. You cannot deceive or defraud the Lord. You deceive no one but yourself.

* * *

9. The secret of success in the Path is "Bhajan, more Bhajan, and still more Bhajan." (Practice, more Practice and still more Practice).

With Bhajan only for three hours, the scale will always weigh heavily on the worldly side. You ought to become wholly and solely God-minded. Throughout the day, no matter in what occupation you are engaged, the soul and the mind must constantly look up to Him at the eye centre. All the twenty-four hours of the day, there must be a yearning to meet the Lord, a continuous pang of separation from Him. Nay, every moment, whether eating, drinking, walking, awake or asleep you must have His Name on your lips and His form before your eyes.

For the past countless ages we have been separated from Him and have been wantonly wandering out. We have been so much chained and dragged by the mind and illusion that we have completely forgotten the Lord and our Divine Origin. We need a complete reorientation. We must tell our mind that in thousands of lives have we acted according to its behests and now we are determined to dedicate this life to God and God alone. Every spare moment must go to Bhajan. Now all our time must be His.

* * *

10.   A young Sadhu is like a young widow. Both should live in a fortress. Your fort is your Guru. Always remain under His protection. Never step out of His Commandments and always remain within the four walls of His teachings. Make Him your rock of refuge and your only sheet-anchor. No harm will then befall you. Within that fortress you should build a 'tower of safety' for your residence. Its four walls would be (1) silence; (2) eating only a small amount of food; (3) wakefulness; (4) solitude.

1.   *Silence*–Much physical and spiritual energy is dissipated by talking. Silence is golden. Speak as little as possible. Open your lips only when it is most necessary. And when you must speak, do so in the most kind and gentle manner. Never lose your temper over anything. You are not running this world. Leave that to Him whose function it is to do so. If a person behaves in a stupid fashion, you need not copy him nor adopt his ways.   Always keep your tongue (the two-edged sword) under control.

2.   *Eating only a small amount of food* –This also relates to the tongue. We eat much more than we require, because it appeals to the palate. One should eat only as much as is necessary to keep body and soul together. We should eat only enough to live in devotion, and not live to eat, as some people seem to

think. A man becomes an angel by eating less, and a beast by eating more. Too much eating and sleeping keep one away from the door of the Lord. Indulgence in these two activities clouds the inner vision.

Keep thy stomach empty.
That God may fill thee with His Love.
Shut your mouth,
That God may open your eyes.

3. *Wakefulness* —Sleep also is correlated to eating. Over-eating always makes one feel sleepy. It makes one sluggish. The less we sleep, the more spiritual prog-ress we can make. We do not need so much sleep as we usually have. A few hours sleep every night is quite sufficient. It leads to inner progress.

4. *Solitude* – (Living alone as much as possible)–To be alone as much as possible is essential for a spiritual seeker. Mixing with people brings us down to the path of the mind. It is the Path of the Master which we seek to follow. "Flee from men and look above thee."

* * *

11. A Satsangi complained of falling asleep during meditation. The Master said: A practitioner (Sadhak) should take advantage of the time when sleep overtakes him. At that time the tendency of the mind is naturally towards the eye centre. So, welcome this sleepy feeling, but do not fall asleep. At the time of meditation you may feel sleepy, but should avoid sleep. Keep awake and fully conscious. Take advantage of this natural tendency of the mind and senses at this time and sit in your eye focus. This state of 'waking sleep' is a blissful state. Practise it for some days and you will find how it helps towards your inner ascent. But care should be taken that you neither fall asleep nor fully wake up. In this state, the mind often becomes one with the Universal Mind and sees many visions and sights.

Do not sleep during or immediately after Bhajan.

* * *

12.   To one who had recently retired on pension, the Master said: "You should look upon this day as your most lucky day. You have played your game well. All your worldly duties have finished. Now you should do something for yourself. Up to this time, you have been doing others' work. Now do your own. All desires and worldly cravings should be turned out from your mind. Tell your mind that you have finished your game in the world and now God's inning begins. Take your mind out from family, children, houses, property, wealth, honour, country and all connections with the world. Bring your mind to such a state that the existence or non-existence of these things may have no effect on you. Now give all your thought, attention and time to God and God alone. Become His now. Cleanse your mind of everything else. Think day and night of Bhajan and of nothing else. Work hard. Fight the mind fearlessly. The Guru is with you. With His help, subdue the mind."

* * *

13.   Much depends upon the type of food we eat. "As we eat, so our mind becomes" and "Our food makes our mind" are old sayings which are very true. Bad (Rajasik or Tamasik)* food gives rise to bad thoughts. Pure (Sattvik)* food will

---

*   *SATTVIK* (relating to Satoguna) food is that which produces tranquillity and pure thoughts. This consists of fruits, vegetables, milk that is not very hot and only in small quantity, butter, cheese, dairy products, honey, almonds, oats, wheat, pulse, rice, etc. It includes all simple light food in small quantities.

*   *RAJASIK* food is that which makes the mind crave worldly activity. It consists of eggs, fish, saffron, pastry, salt, pepper and all stimulating articles, including tea, coffee and hot milk or any food in large quantities.

*   *TAMASIK*   food is that which produces sluggishness, anger, etc. It consists of meat, wine, tobacco and heavy and stale food or too much of anything, and, of course, all alcoholic drinks.

develop pure thoughts. Pure thoughts will create good
character, and good character is most essential for love of
God. Without love of God, there can be no spiritual progress.

Always take pure (sattvik) food. That too should be earned
by honest means, and out of which the right share given to
elders and to all whom it is due. Foods should be light and
simple, and be prepared and eaten in a happy mood, in a
small quantity, after duly thanking the Giver.

* * *

14.   Impure thoughts are a great hindrance to spiritual
uplift. They act as poison. Keep alert and immediately divert
your mind from such thoughts. If you rub an itch, it will
eventually become a malignant boil.

* * *

15.   Always keep your mind in Simran. Does it cost
anything? Just go on repeating the Holy Names as the small
boys repeat, "one, two, three, four." Simran is a great force.
By Simran alone, you develop strong will power. Simran
should be done patiently and vigorously, without a break. It
should be incessant, unceasing, continuous and constant.

* * *

16.   A Satsangi complained: "Sir, my mind does not
allow me to sit in Bhajan, and when I sit, it makes me forget
Simran."

The Master smiled and said: Well, what else should it do?
It is doing its duty most faithfully. Should you not do yours?
Attack it with full force. At this stage, it is a fierce battle
between mind and soul. Never give any quarter to the mind.
The best way is to open the attack first and to go on repeating
it, so that it may never find any time to return the attack.

* * *

17.   Meditation should be done with the attention fully concentrated at the eye centre. It is the 'attention' that is to do the Simran, while the body, mind, tongue, the power of seeing and the power of hearing are motionless and at rest.

* * *

18.   Satsangis should form the habit of 'thinking' – clear thinking. Very few people 'think'. Why do we lose our temper? Because we do not reflect. Why do people fall prey to the attack of lust? Because they do not think. Why does a mother weep at the death of her son ? Why do people commit suicide at the loss of property or wealth? Because they do not think. 'Vichar' (clear thinking) is ninety per cent 'Abhyas'. Clear thinking is a blessing. It can easily be attained by a little practice. Most of our actions are done on the spur of the moment, without thinking. Always reflect calmly. If you knew how much harm anger does to your liver and heart, you would never lose your temper over anything. Ask a physician and he will tell you how blood becomes poisoned in a fit of anger.

* * *

19.   Did worry ever help to solve any problem? It is born of confused thinking. Form the habit of clear thinking always and laugh away your troubles and sorrows. Even the devil himself can do nothing to a man so long as he can laugh. Does a laugh cost anything? It is as easy to laugh as to worry and fret. Only a little effort is required in the beginning. It becomes a habit after a time. Your worrying shows that you have no faith in the goodness of God or even in God Himself. Let Him accomplish things in His own way rather than in the way that you desire. Try to adjust yourself to all that He does and you will never be unhappy.

* * *

20.   A wound inflicted on the body with a sharp weapon heals up in time, but not so the wound that the tongue inflicts on the heart of a man. Beware of hurting the feelings of any living being. This should be given as much importance as the vows of abstinence from meat, etc., that we take at the time of Initiation. Bhajan and Abhyas (meditation and spiritual practice) are impossible without following a strict code of discipline. The vow of abstinence from animal food is intended to impress upon the mind the idea of Ahimsa—harmlessness or non-injury by thought, word or deed. Remember that life is dear to all. Patanjali Rishi has laid down 'Five Dont's' (Yam) and 'Five Do's' (Niyams) in his 'Yog Shastra' to be observed by the practitioners of Yoga. They form very good rules of conduct and may be profitably followed by Satsangis. The five Yams are :

1. *Ahimsa*—not to injure any living creature by thought, word or deed.
2. *Satya*—not to tell a lie, *i.e.,* truthfulness in thought, word and deed.
3. *Asteya* —not to steal; never to desire or take what is not yours.
4. *Brahmcharya*—not to look upon sex with lust, in thought, word or deed, *i.e.,* chastity, continence and conservation of sexual energy.
5. *Aparigraha*—negation of desire for possession; not possessing unnecessary articles; renunciation.

The following are the five Niyams :

1. *Shouch* —cleanliness.
2. *Santosh* —contentment.
3. *Tap* —self-discipline by voluntary submission.
4. *Swadhyaya*—study of religious books.
5. *Ishwar Pranidhan* —unshakable faith in God and complete surrender to Him. Effort at God-realization.

* * *

21. In a Satsang, the Master was describing the gran-
deur and the glory of the wonderful Radiant Form of the
Master within. A Satsangi stood up and complained: "Master!
I used to see daily your Radiant Form, but it has not appeared
for a month." Master said, "Some grief or pleasure must have
assailed your mind". The Satsangi replied, "Yes, Sir–I have
lost my only son." The Master replied, "Master is always
there; when by concentration our mind ascends high, it gets
His Darshan (sees Him) but when it is disturbed, it falls
down and cannot see Him. Did dwelling on grief ever solve
any problem, or did worry ever help anybody? Attend to
Bhajan and Simran, which alone are the source of peace,
pleasure and happiness."

* * *

22. To lead a good, pure, moral life in youth one needs
the courage, bravery and resolve of a prophet.

* * *

23. You want me to define a True Master and tell what
He gives? Well, the perfect Master is a Man-God or God-Man.
He is a human being, in whose person the Lord of the
Universe, the Eternal Sat Nam, the Everlasting Shabd comes
to reside on earth. He is the 'Word' turned into flesh. The Lord
leaves His Palace, conceals Himself in human garb and goes
out in search of His son to the habitation of gypsies who have
kidnapped him. He lives amongst them and leads the life they
lead. His son does not recognize Him. Nobody believes what
He says. With great difficulty He prevails upon His child to
accompany Him to His Palace to see for Himself, with his own
eyes, what great heritage by right belongs to him. From a
gypsy hamlet, He brings him to the Royal Palace and offers
him the Throne, and does not leave him till he is safely settled
in the Palace.

* * *

24. Happy is he whose wants are few. The fewer the wants, the happier the person. "Who doth not want many things, is the king of kings." It is our wants that make us poor. One who has no wants is the richest person. During his sojourn in India, Alexander the Great went to see a Sadhu living on the banks of the river Beas, about whose supernatural powers he had heard a great deal. He found him sitting on a palm leaf under an umbrella made of banyan tree leaves. This was all that the Sadhu possessed. On being informed that he had passed all his life there and had remained there even in torrential rain, burning heat or piercing cold, Alexander offered to build a house for him. This he refused, saying "Why build a house? Are we to live here forever?" Then Alexander asked if he could do anything else for him. "Yes, please see that none of the your men comes to me," he said. Alexander offered to give half his kingdom at the time of his death, to anyone who could make him live just for as much time as would enable him to see his mother. But the physicians replied that, even if he gave the whole of his kingdom, they could not add one single breath to his life. Tears welled up in the king's eyes, and with a deep sigh he said, "Alas! Had I known that a breath was so costly a thing, I would never have wasted them in useless pursuits." Then he directed that, during his funeral procession, his hands should be kept out of his coffin with palms upwards so that the world might take a lesson from the Great Alexander, who had planned to conquer the world, but was going away from it empty-handed.

* * *

25. I cannot lay adequate stress on living a pure moral life. High moral character is most essential for spiritual progress. Nam and Kam (lust) cannot exist together. They are as antagonistic to each other, as light is to darkness. Where there is Kam, Nam does not enter. And when Nam comes, Kam vanishes. A Satsangi should be an example to the world. His eyes should radiate purity and a spiritual fragrance should issue forth from his body. Avoid the life of sensual pleasures, and turn out desire for lust from your heart. A life of virtue, peace and contentment is possible only when you rise above the nine doors of the body. To indulge in sex pleasures and to expect to enter the Kingdom of Heaven is sheer mockery. For such a one that door shall never open.

* * *

26. The Astral Form of the Master is so Radiant, Beautiful and Magnetic that, after seeing It, one does not find any form or figure as beautiful in this world and so gives up all worldly attachments. A deep consuming love for the Lord and a burning pang of separation from Him are most essential for His Darshan. The fire of Love burns away all impurities. Only desire to meet the Beloved remains.

* * *

27. Never speak ill of others. It is a great sin. There may be some pleasure or enjoyment in other sins, but tell me what pleasure there is in 'slander'? Sheikh Saadi, the famous sage of Shiraz says, "If I were to speak ill of anybody, I would speak ill of my own mother; for if the merits of my good deeds are to go to any person, let them go to my own mother." Maharaj Ji (Baba Sawan Singh Ji) used to say that all the good deeds of one who talks ill of another are credited to the account of the slandered one. The slanderer washes away our sins without charging us anything.

* * *

28. How profusely we thank those at whose hands we have received some small favours! Parents and teachers inculcate into their charges the rules of good conduct; but sadly enough, the children are starved of spiritual nourishment in their formative years. What greater lacuna in their training can there be than the ignorance of God--the

fountain of all Goodness and reservoir of all gifts? When
this basic perspective is missing, life is full of confusion and
bewilderment and traditions of respectful behaviour and
unimpeachable morality decline. It is the duty of parents to tell
their children of God and things divine to enable them to
develop a healthy sense of values and lay the foundations of
a virtuous life.

* * *

29. This life is but a link in an infinite chain of existence. The body perishes but the soul lives on—immortal,
treading the path back from its painful separation and prodi-
gality to its blissful return to the mansions of the Lord. Says
Dadu, the great Rajasthani Saint:

> I was when the world was not.
> I shall be when the world would cease to be.

* * *

30. Do not indulge in idle, frivolous talk. If you are
conscious of your spiritual poverty, devote every minute to
becoming worthier to receive your rich heritage. Mere light-
hearted gossip (frivolity) makes a mockery of your prayers
before the Lord. It brands you a hypocrite and cuts at the very
roots of spirituality.

Extravagant spending of precious time and energy is
incompatible with your pleading for Grace. Think more, and
talk less.

* * *

31. Complaints often reach me from satsangis that the
mind does not allow them to sit in meditation. They are too
prone to yield to its suggestions. If the spirit is unwilling and
the flesh is weak, where lies the remedy? At the slightest
discomfort caused by maintenance of the posture and withdrawal of the soul current, the mind urges the practitioner to

give up meditation. Let us remember the unfailing verdict: 'No pain, no gain'. Only the most valiant of fighters, who are prepared to embrace death (closing the nine doors to worldly satisfactions), and storm the dark fortress of Kal and Karmas, can achieve their purpose. Listen to what lovers say: "O Farid! (In my effort to reach His Palace) my body is afire like an oven and my bones are burning like fuel. (Shall I tarry ? No.) When my legs are withered and move no more, I shall walk on my head, if I could have only a glimpse of Him."

* * *

32. In Satsang, an American lady inquired about Karmas and Sanskaras. Master replied:

1. Karmas are our actions or deeds and also their reaction or retribution–a self-operating law of cause and effect. None can escape the result of his deeds. You shall have to reap what you have sown.

2. Sanskaras are tendencies inherent (but latent) in a man as a result of his past Karmas, left as residue from his previous incarnations and affecting and shaping his actions in the present life.

* * *

33. The same lady put some questions about the function of reason and intellect in the search after Truth and God. Master said, "Listen carefully! Intellect was given to us by our Creator to carry on the work of this world (of phenomena) only. Intellect is the faculty which enables us to analyse and retain the salient impressions of worldly experiences, in the light of which we can act with advantage. When the scope of activity of the intellect is so limited, how can it perceive the profound spiritual reality? For worldly experiences are associated with the nine doors that lead without; whereas the realm of the spirit lies within the Tenth gate. Again with environment and tradition, age and clime, likes and dislikes, the reasoning process shows marked variations. A Russian and American, a young man and an old one, think in ways that are quite apart. In lust and anger, how grotesquely convulsed are a man's thoughts?"

"When this yardstick of reason is always changing, what reliance can be placed on its measurements ?"

"Then, on what should we rely for God-realization?" inquired the lady. Master said, "God-realization commences when the aspirant closes the nine outlets and turns his back upon this world to journey within." The inner experiences and their comprehension are beyond the ken of intellect. The soul alone perceives them. No intellectual wizardry can unravel the mystery; but the soul sees and knows the naked reality, the Truth. A spark of the Divine itself, it can understand the Divine and Limitless as its consciousness enlarges; and when God-realization is consummated, the soul has united with its source.

Do not, therefore, expect this feeble, limited intellect to understand the spiritual subtleties by a mere play of reasoning. Even in the field of worldly phenomena, so much eludes our grasp. What shall we say of the worlds beyond the senses? Suppose a baby asks its mother, "Mummy how was I born?" Mamma knows the answer, but also knows that the baby would not understand. She laughs and says, "I bought you for a farthing from a gipsy girl."

* * *

34. A lady whose son was flying to Europe for studies approached the Master and said, "Sir, I am very worried these days." Master inquired the cause of her worry. She said, "My son is flying to Europe for further studies tomorrow." Master just smiled a little (there was always a laugh on his lips) and said, "Well, what is there to worry? Is it his flying or further studies or tomorrow?" The lady also laughed and said, "Sir, my heart sinks when I think of the dangers of flying."

Master: "Why not think of the comfort, convenience and quick arrival at the destination?"

Then Master remarked, "This is how man creates worries for himself. Ninety-nine per cent of our worries are self created and quite groundless." He quoted a line from Shakespeare,which says that the dread of a coming misfortune makes us more miserable than the actual misfortune, which may come or may not come at all.

* * *

35. Our love for the Lord requires constant feeding. Like fire, it is apt to die out without fuel. Bhajan and Simran is the fuel that sustains this fire. So never miss Bhajan for a single day. One day's negligence in Bhajan retards the progress of the journey by one month.

* * *

36. Life is not worth worrying over too much. It begins in folly and ends in smoke. It has to come to an end one day whether you like it or not. And its middle portion also passes away. The best policy is to laugh its worries away.

* * *

37. A young girl who had recently lost her husband was so much overwhelmed with grief that she requested the Master to put an end to her life. 'I want to die, Sir,' she said. 'Well!' replied the Master, "Will your death put an end to your Karmas which have brought about this agony? No. You will carry these along with you in your next birth. Then why not pay off the debt now instead of adding another sin—the greatest of all sins, suicide–to the already heavy debt of karmas?"

* * *

38. My friends! On this Path, it is most essential to toil hard. Unless one puts in all the effort and labour that lies in one's power, and pushes hard, the door will not open.

* * *

39. Our prayers and pleadings are quite useless, unless these are supported by all the effort on our part to push the door open. The Master knows that we are only feigning thirst and desire for Nam. Our prayers are not sincere and true. Our mind is still steeped in cravings for the world and its objects. It is submerged in lust and greed. It is running after name and fame. It constantly lives in vanity and pride. Remember that a Master cannot be deceived or cheated. Unless the yearning to meet Him is intense and true, He remains silent and unattentive.

* * *

40. So long as a baby is busy with its dolls and satisfied with its toys, the mother also does not worry about it, but as soon as it throws away its playthings and wants nothing but its mother, the mother cannot resist its cries and comes running to take it in her lap. Likewise so long as we lean on others He lets us do so, but when after repeated disappointments, we surrender to Him completely, regarding Him as our only sheet-anchor, He comes to our succor instantly.

* * *

41. Where is the difficulty in doing Simran (repetition of Holy Names)? Does it cost anything? Have you to carry any load or burden on your head? Or have you to face a bullet or a gun shot? What is the trouble in it? Just sit comfortably in a chair and go on repeating the Names mentally.

A voice: "Sir, the mind wanders away."

Master: "All right, Let it wander. You go on doing your Simran."

"Every moment spent in His memory is credited to your account. Twice daily, read two or three Shabds (poems) from Sar Bachan or from some other Sant Mat literature. This will be of great help."

* * *

42. All the actions of the devotees are opposite to the ways of the world. To see the Beloved they shut their eyes. People desire wealth; they love poverty. People run after pleasure; they seek pain. People adore life; they love death.

* * *

43. Write on the gates of all temples and mosques that the Lord resides in the heart of man, away from religions and creeds.

* * *

44. Master's Form will appear in the heart only when all desires of the world are turned out of it.

* * *

45. Replying to a European Satsangi, Master said: "Saints do not encourage showing of miracles or using spiritual powers towards worldly ends. It is not difficult for an advanced Satsangi to cure a disease or give eyesight to the blind or to raise the dead, but why should it be done against the decree of the Lord? They have no vanity to feed nor an axe of their own to grind. They want the Lord to rule and not themselves. You all know the story of Baba Atal, the nine year

old son of Guru Hargobind Ji. When he went to the house of
his friend, Mohan, to get his turn of the play that was left
over the previous evening, he found him lying on the ground,
with his parents and family members weeping around him. He
was told that the boy was dead. Atal said, 'No he is not dead.
He is feigning death to cheat me of my turn of the game.'
Taking him by the hand, Atal made him stand up and took
him out to the playground. When Guru Hargobind Sahib
heard of this, he summoned his son before him and said,
'Now, child! For showing this miracle, either you shall
have to leave the world or I shall have to go.' The boy
agreed himself to suffer for his indiscretion and lay down
on the ground then and there and breathed his last. You all
have seen his white marble mausoleum near the Golden
Temple at Amritsar. Huzur Maharaj Ji (Baba Sawan Singh
Ji) used to say that these Ridhis and Sidhis (supernatural
powers) are like prostitutes in the way of Satsangis and
try to rob him of all his earnings. Beware of them always.'

* * *

46. "The path of true love is never smooth," says
Shakespeare. The truer the love, the rougher the road. This is
also true in the case of love for the Lord. The more you love
Him, the more difficulties and trials He puts in your way.
Gold, to be pure, must be put in the fire. Paltu Sahib says,
"Love is not an easy affair. Are you willing to cut your head
with your own hands? If not, then do not dream of love. It is
not a sugar cube that you will swallow. A lover remains
hanging on the cross all day and night. He dies while living and
gives up all desires for body and life. Not a single drop of blood
is left in him. Neither does he cry, nor does a sigh ever escape
his heart. Renouncing all honour and pride, he even starves
himself of food and sleep. Paltu! How foolish they are who
become lovers, thinking it a feast in their aunty's home."

* * *

47.   How we waste our precious human lives in running after sense pleasures, which bring only distress, disease, agony and pain in their wake. In fact, we do not seem to realize the great value of this precious gift which the merciful Lord has bestowed upon us. We get the human body after passing through milllions of lives in lower species. As worms, birds and beasts, we had father, mother, wife and children. Love, hate, lust, hunger and greed we experienced even then. What then is the superiority of man? Our Benign Creator's main purpose in giving us intelligence was that we may know ourselves and seek and meet our Creator in this life. If we fail to do that, we are no better than beasts. Let us then avail of this gift in realizing God.

* * *

48.   Tendency of evil is downward. A single evil thought will bring one down from the celestial heights of Brahmand to the lowest region of Hades. As a man slips down from a snowy peak, so does a lustful thought pulls down a devotee. Lust and love of the Lord are a pair of opposites. They cannot co-exist in a heart. Where lust is, the Lord's love is not and where the Lord's love pervades, lust makes itself completely scarce.

* * *

49.   Distress, disease, sorrow and sickness are great chasteners. They make us human beings and bring us nearer to God. Lord Krishna says to Udho (in Bhagvat): I make three rare gifts to my most beloved devotees. They are: *(i)* poverty, *(ii)* illness and *(iii)* dishonour. Lord Jesus Christ truly said that it was easier for a camel to pass through the eye of a needle than for a rich man to enter the Kingdom of Heaven. Lord Krishna named love of body, vanity, pride, and attachment to worldly possessions as hindrances to God-realization.

* * *

GLOSSARY

A

abhyas   Spiritual practice; spiritual exercise.

abhyasi   One who performs spiritual exercise.

adi   Primal; first; original.

Adi Granth *or* **Adi Granth Sahib**   Literally, primal scripture, also called the "Granth Sahib"; name given to the scripture that enshrines the hymns of the first five Gurus and the ninth Guru in the line of Guru Nanak, and numerous other saints from various parts of India, which makes it a lucid mosaic of esoteric poetry of saints with a variety of religious, cultural, vocational, and geographic backgrounds. The Adi Granth was compiled by Guru Arjun, the fifth Guru, who, representing the universal outlook of all true saints, gave it a broad base and acceptability. Ever since its inception the followers of the Gurus have adopted the Adi Granth as their most sacred scripture.

adi karma   Original (*adi*) action causing reaction (*karma*); karma of the beginning, not earned by the individual, but established by the Creator in the beginning. See also: karma.

Agam Lok   Inaccessible (*agam*) region (*lok*); the name of the seventh spiritual region. Agam Purush is the Supreme Being presiding over Agam Lok.

ahankar   Ego or I-ness; one of the five deadly passions (lust, anger, greed, attachment, ego); pride and vanity; also one of the four divisions of mind, its function is to separate self and self-interests from all else, which leads to erroneous identification with faces and objects of the world. See also: antashkaran.

ahimsa   Nonviolence, not hurting any living being, by either word or act.

Ahura Mazda Ancient Persian name for the lord of life (*ahura*) and lord of wisdom (*mazda*), specially in Zoroastrianism.

Akal Timeless; beyond birth and death.

Akal Purush Timeless (*akal*) being (*purush*); the one who is beyond the sphere of birth and death; the supreme positive power, as opposed to Kal, the negative power.

akash Literally, "sky" or "heaven"; ether, the highest of the five elements, which remains dormant in all living forms except the human. See also: tattwa.

Akash Bani Sound or voice (*bani*) from the sky (*akash*); heavenly music; Word or Logos; audible life stream. See also: Shabd.

akshar Indelible; imperishable; Akshar Purush is the appellation for God, the creative power.

Alakh Lok Invisible (*alakh*) region (*lok*); the sixth spiritual region. Alakh Purush is the Lord of Alakh Lok.

Allah The Arabic name for God.

Anaahat *or* **Anahat Shabd** Unstruck (*anahat*) Sound (*shabd*).

Anhad *or* **Anhad Shabd** Limitless (*anahad*) Sound (*shabd*): the Word or divine creative power. Also called the unstruck sound, logos. See also: Shabd.

Anami Lok Nameless (*anami*) region (*lok*); the eighth spiritual region, presided over by Anami Purush, Radha Soami, the Supreme Being.

And *or* **Anda** Literally, "egg"; the astral region, the grand division of the creation lying immediately above the physical realm, Pind.

andi man astral mind.

antashkaran *or* **antahkaran** Literally, internal (antar) instruments (karan). Indian philosophy has described four internal-instruments through which cognitive functions are performed: mind (*man*), intellect (*buddhi*), reflective aspect of intellect (*chitt or chit*), and egotism or erroneous identification (*ahankar*).

Anurag Sagar Believed to be written by Kabir, it is a book of verse in the form of a dialogue between Kabir and his disciple Dharam Das. Modern scholars maintain that this book was written by Dharam Das and not Kabir, and can be described as the sayings of Kabir according to Dharam Das.

Arjun Dev See: Guru Nanak.

Arjuna One of the Pandavas and the hero of the Mahabharata. It was to him that Lord Krishna taught the doctrines known as Bhagvadgita.

asana Posture; in spiritual practice, a meditative pose, with body erect, mind in poise.

Ashtdal Kanwal Eight-petalled (*ashtdal*) lotus (*kanwal*); the name of the centre beyond the eye centre where the disciple first meets the Radiant Form of the Master.

astral region That part of the subtle universe which lies above the physical worlds; the first spiritual region, known as Sahasradal Kanwal.

asura Demons. Asura Lok, the region of demons. In the oldest portions of the Rig Veda, Asura is used for the supreme spirit; later, *sura* came to mean "gods," and *asura*, "demons," "enemies of God."

atma Soul or spirit. See also: paramatma, jivatma.

atma pad Spirit world, referring generally to the astral plane or first region; more technically, refers to Daswan Dwar, the third spiritual region, where the soul gains self-realization.

aum See: om.

awagawan Coming and going; refers to age-long cycles of births and deaths; transmigration, reincarnation. See also: chaurasi.

B

Baba Jaimal Singh Ji Maharaj The name of the founder of the Radha Soami colony at Beas (Punjab). He was a devoted and highly advanced disciple of Soami Ji Maharaj and was appointed by him in 1877 to carry on the spiritual work with headquarters in the Punjab. He left this world on 29 December, 1903. Several months before he departed, he appointed Huzur Maharaj Baba Sawan Singh Ji as his successor. It was the latter who named the place Dera Baba Jaimal Singh, in honor of his Satguru. In his sacred memory, a *bhandara* is held annually on 29 December at the colony at Beas. He was born in village Ghoman (Punjab) in July, 1839.

Baba Ji   Same as Baba Jaimal Singh Ji Maharaj.

babu   A title equivalent to Mister or Esquire.

bachan   Word; discourse; saying; instruction; order; command.

Bahisht   Paradise; the same as Baikunth and Swarg.

Baikunth, Baikuntha, *or* **Baikunth Lok**   The abode of Vishnu; the same as Bahisht and Swarg.

Bani   Voice, word or teachings; the Voice or Word of God; the audible life stream. See also: Shabd.

Beas   The name of a small village, situated on the banks of the Beas river in Punjab.

Bhagvadgita   Literally, "The Song of the Lord." It embodies the teachings of Lord Krishna, given in the dialogue between Krishna and Arjuna on the battlefield, and is the most popular book on Hindu philosophy.

bhajan   Worship or spiritual practice; listening to the melody of the Shabd within. Also used as an expression of outer devotional songs.

bhakt, bhakta, *or* **bhagat**   Devotee.

bhakti   Devotion.

bhakti marg   The path (*marg*) of devotion (*bhakti*). See also: prem marg.

bhandara   Religious feast; large scale feeding of people; esoterically the internal spiritual feast.

Bhanwar Gupha   Revolving (*bhanwar*) Cave (*gupha*); the name of the fourth spiritual region.

bibek   See: vivek.

bina *or* **been**   See: vina.

bodhisattva   One who is on the way to attainment of perfect knowledge and has only a certain number of births to undergo before attaining the state of a supreme Buddha.

Brahm   The ruler of Trikuti, the second spiritual region; known also as the ruler of Brahm Lok, the name given to the Three Worlds; regarded by many as the Supreme Being.

Brahma   God of creation in the Hindu trinity of creator, preserver, destroyer (Brahma, Vishnu, Shiva).

brahmacharya   The practice of celibacy, remaining continent.

Brahmand *or* **Brahmanda**   Literally, "egg of Brahm"; the grand division of the creation extending from Anda up to Bhanwar Gupha; the entire universe over which Brahm has jurisdiction.

brahmandi   Pertaining to Brahmand; universal.

brahmandi manas   Universal mind, which rules the subtle worlds, such as heaven, hell, etc.

brahmin   A member of the highest of the four Hindu castes; a priest.

buddh, budh, *or* **buddhi**   Intellect; one of the four phases of mind. See also: antashkaran.

Buddha   The great sage, Prince Siddhartha of the Sakya clan. The religion of Buddhism is based on his teachings.

C

causal region   See: Trikuti.

chakra   Wheel; centre; ganglion; any of the six energy centres in the human body, with parts resembling the petals of a lotus. See also: kanwal.

chaurasi   Eighty-four; the wheel of eighty-four, or the wheel of transmigration. The name indicates the concept in Indian mythology and Hindu scriptures of eight million, four hundred thousand species in the creation. Mystics have adopted this phrase to tell of the multiplicity of births that souls pass through in the creation, according to the law of karma. See also: karma, awagawan.

chela   Disciple.

chetan   Conscious; awakened; spirit; conscious living as opposed to *jar* (inert or inanimate); reason; soul; self; intelligence; wisdom; also called Chaitanya.

Chetan Akash   The heavenly region above the eyes; part of the first region of spirituality.

Chidakash   The same as Chetan Akash.

chit, chitt, *or* **chitta**   Reflective aspect of intellect; one of the four divisions of mind; the faculty of remembering anddiscerning beauty, form and color. See also: antashkaran.

D

Dadu (1544-1603):   A saint of Rajputana, well known for his bold utterances in his beautiful poetry.

dama   Restraining or subduing the passions, curbing the mind.

dand   Self-discipline; punishment; law of life.

darshan   Vision, sight or seeing; implies looking intently at the Master with a deep feeling of respect, devotion and one-pointed attention.

Daswan Dwar   Literally, the tenth door; an appellation of the third spiritual region. Trikuti is said to have an inner *garh* (citadel) having ten gates, nine of which are open. The tenth, that leads to the third region, is closed; hence, the third region itself is called Daswan Dwar. In fact, both Sunn and Maha Sunn are referred to as Daswan Dwar—Sunn being the region itself, and Maha Sunn, being the region of intense darkness between Daswan Dwar and Bhanwar Gupha (the fourth region).

daya   Mercy; grace.

dayal   Compassionate one; a term for the Supreme Being, the positive and merciful power, as opposed to Kal, the lord of judgment, who metes out relentless justice.

Dera   Camp or colony. In this book the name refers to the Radha Soami colony, situated on the banks of the river Beas, in the Punjab.

Dera Baba Jaimal Singh   P.O. address of Radha Soami colony, Beas.

desh   Country or region; inner region. See also: Sat Desh.

Dev Lok   Region of the gods.

deva *or* **devta**   Shining ones; personifications of the forces of nature; gods, angels.

dham   Region or abode; place or home. See also: Radha Soami Dham.

Dharam Rai   Literally, "King Judge," the lord of justice, who administers reward or punishment to the soul after death, according to its own actions during life.

dharma Righteousness or duty; moral and religious duty in life; also used as a synonym for "religion."

dharma megha A particular state of concentration (*samadhi*) which frees the mind from all activity, inward or outward; a person in such a state is said to radiate a light like a mantle of glory.

dhun Sound or melody; the Word; the heavenly music. See also: Shabd.

dhunatmak, dhunatmik, or dhunyatmak nam The inexpressible primal sound, which cannot be written or spoken or heard with the physical ears; the inner music which can be experienced only by the soul. See also: Shabd.

dhyan Inner contemplation. A meditation technique taught by saints in which the devotee contemplates on the form of the Master within.

din dayal *Din* means "humble"; *dayal* means "merciful"; hence, "merciful to the humble."

Dwapar Yuga The Copper Age, the third yuga in the cycle of the ages. See also: yuga.

F

faqir *or* **fakir** Arabic term for a holy man; an ascetic or a religious mendicant.

G

Ganges *or* **Ganga** A sacred river in India. Many places of pilgrimage are situated on the banks of this river.

Ghat Ramayana Name of a book by Tulsi Sahib of Hathras. It is written in beautiful poetry and is strictly an epic of the soul, as distinguished from the Ramayana by Tulsi Das, who lived in another age. Ghat Ramayana pertains to the ascent of the soul within.

Gita See Bhagvadgita.

Granth A book, especially a religious scripture; the Sikh scriptures.

Granth Sahib A title of respect given by the Sikhs to the Adi Granth. See also: Adi Granth.

guna   Attribute or quality; there are three attributes or qualities of primordial matter (*prakriti*) out of which the creation proceeds (harmony, action, and inertia), the source of which is in Trikuti. See also: satogun, rajogun, tamogun.

gurbani   Literally, "teachings of the Guru," esoterically, Nam, Shabd, or Word. Also means what has been written in the Granth Sahib; teachings of the saints; sometimes a particular book, such as the Granth Sahib, Sar Bachan, etc., is also referred to as Gurbani.

gurbhakta   Devotee of a Guru.

gurbhakti   Devotion to a Guru.

Gurdwara   The name used by the Sikhs for their house of worship.

Gurmat   Teachings of the Guru; same as Sant Mat.

gurmukh   One whose face is turned towards the Guru; one who has completely surrendered to the Guru as opposed to one who is slave to the mind (*manmukh*); a highly advanced soul; a term sometimes used for a saint or perfect Master.

gurmukhta   The quality of being a *gurmukh*; devotion and surrender to the Guru; obedience.

Gurmukhi   Punjabi language, so called because it was the language of Guru Nanak.

Guru   Master; teacher; spiritual enlightener.

Guru Granth Sahib   See: Adi Granth.

Guru Nanak (1469-1539):   He was born at Talwandi, near Lahore (now in Pakistan). His parents were Kalu and Tripta. Guru Nanak condemned the orthodox creed of the people with great vigor, and he laid emphasis on the spiritual aspect of religion and on love of God and man. He undertook four major tours to propagate his teachings. The following were his successors to the mastership:

Guru Angad (1504-1552): Second in the line of succession.

Guru Amardas (1479-1574): Third in the line of succession.

Guru Ramdas (1534-1581): Fourth in the line of succession.

Guru Arjan Dev (1563-1606): Fifth in the line of succession.

Guru Hargovind (1595-1644): Sixth in the line of succession.

Guru Har Rai (1630-1661): Seventh in the line of succession.

Guru Harkishan (1656-1664): Eighth in the line of succession.

Guru Tegh Bahadur (1621-1675): Ninth in the line of succession.

Guru Gobind Singh (1666-1708): Tenth in the line of succession.

gyan   Knowledge; True knowledge; spiritual knowledge; spiritual wisdom; spiritual enlightenment.

gyani   A learned person; one who practices or walks on the path of knowledge and wisdom (*gyan*).

gyan marg   The path or way (*marg*) of learning. See also: bhakti marg.

gyan yoga   That form of yoga which attempts to achieve God-realization through the acquisition of knowledge. See also: gyan marg.

H

Hafiz   A famous poet-saint of Persia.

Haq   Literally, truth; Arabic designation of the fifth spiritual region.

Hazrat Mohammed   Prophet and founder of Islam.

hansa   Swan; symbolic of purity, the name given to the highly evolved souls in the regions beyond Brahm; the less-evolved souls are often likened to crows.

Hardwar   A place of pilgrimage. It is from this place that the Ganges, coming from the mountains, gathers volume and flows out into the plains. Orthodox Hindus immerse the ashes of their departed relatives into the river at this place, believing that this will secure salvation for the departed ones.

hatha yoga   One of the Indian systems of yoga, which deals only with the physical body.

Huzur *or* **Hazur**   Term of respect used in addressing or applied to kings, holy men, and high personages.

I

ida *or* **ira**   See: sushumna or Shah Rag.

Ism-i-Azam   The greatest Name; Shabd; Sound; inner music; Word.

J

Japji Sahib   The first portion of the Granth Sahib, which consists of the sayings of Guru Nanak and which contains the essence of the entire Granth Sahib.

jat   A caste in modern India, following mostly the agricultural and military professions.

ji   An honorific term which indicates respect and endearment.

jiv *or* **jiva**   Any living being; the individual or unliberated soul; sometimes used to denote human beings generally.

jivan mukti   Salvation while alive, spiritual liberation during this lifetime.

jivatma   Soul embodied in the physical form.

jnana yoga   See: gyan yoga.

jot *or* **jyoti**   Light, flame; refers to the light of the first spiritual region, Sahasradal Kanwal.

K

Kabir Sahib   A well-known saint (1398-1518) who lived in Benares (Kashi), and preached and practiced Surat Shabd Yoga. He condemned the follies and the external observances of Hindus and Muslims alike. He was succeeded by Dharam Das.

Kal   Time or death; the negative power; the universal mind; the ruler of the three perishable worlds (physical, astral, causal); also called Dharam Rai, the lord of judgment, and Yama, the lord of death. Kal's headquarters are in the second spiritual region, Trikuti, of which he is the ruler. Another name for Brahm.

Kalma   Arabic for Bani; Word; Shabd.

Kalyug *or* **Kalyuga**   The fourth cycle of Time, known as the Dark Age or the Iron Age. It is the age in which we live now. See Yuga.

kam   Lust, passion, desire; one of the five passions (lust, anger, greed, attachment, ego). See also: krodh, lobh, moh, ahankar

karam kanda   Rituals, rites, ceremonies, and outward practices in the various religions.

karan   Causual; cause.

karan man   The Casual Mind, which rules the casual region and extends to the top of Brahm.

karan sharir   Causal body; also called seed body (*bij sharir*), because the seeds of all karmas reside in it; all such actions or karmas manifest in the lower astral and physical body. The causal bodycorresponds to the causal region. See also: Trikuti.

karma   Action; the law of action and reaction; the debits and credits resulting from our deeds, which bring us back to the world in future lives to reap their fruits. There are three types of karma: *pralabdh* or *prarabdh karma,* the fate or destiny we experience in the present life which has been shaped by certain of our past actions; *kriyaman karma,* the debits and credits created by our actions in this life, to be reaped in future lives; *sinchit* or *sanchit karma,* the balance of unpaid karmas from all our past lives, the store of karmas.

Karvat   The name of the saw at Benares. The priests in charge claimed that anyone who had his head cut off by it would go to heaven. This practice has been stopped.

khat chakras   The six centres of ganglia in the body.

khat sampatti   The six types of riches, or moral and spiritual wealth:

1. Sama—balance or equanimity.
2. Dama—self-restraint.
3. Uparati—freedom from ceremonial worship.
4. Titiksha—patience.
5. Sharaddha—faith.
6. Samadhanta—deep meditation.

kanwal *or* **kamal**   Lotus; an image used to describe the energy centres, both in the physical body and in the inner regions. See also: chakra; Sahasradal Kanwal.

Kqran   Same as Quran.

Krishna   Lord Krishna, held to be a complete incarnation of Lord Vishnu. He delivered the celebrated Song of the Lord, called Bhagvadgita.

Kritya Yuga   Same as Sat Yuga.

kriyaman   Karma created in the present life. See also: karma.

krodh   Anger; one of the five deadly passions (lust, anger, greed, attachment, and ego). See also: kam, lobh, moh, ahankar.

kundalini   Coiled energy situated at the base of the spine, above the lowest centre (*mul chakra*). When aroused, it rises up through the central canal of the spine, unwinding serpentlike; a practice to be shunned by satsangis, as it can easily dissipate spiritual energy and cause illness, insanity or death.

L

laya yoga   A form of yoga in which the disciple merges his individuality in that of the Guru or Shabd.

lobh   Greed, one of the five deadly passions (lust, anger, greed, attachment, and ego). See also: kam, krodh, moh, ahankar.

lok   Region; world.

M

magi   The wise men of the East; priests of ancient Persia.

maha   Great.

Mahabharat *or* **Mahabharata**   The great epic poem of ancient India, the leading subject of which is the great war between the Kauravas and the Pandavas. The object of the great struggle was the kingdom whose capital was Hastinapur, fifty-seven miles northeast of Delhi. See: Pandavas.

Mahadev *or* **Mahadeo**   The third of the Hindu Triad; the same as Shiva.

Maha Kal   Ruler of the upper part of Brahmand; same as Kal.

maha nada   Great music; the inner music, or audible life stream.

Maha Sunn   The region of intense darkness, situated above Sunn or Daswan Dwar proper, and below Bhanwar Gupha. It is really one of the six great spiritual regions, but the saints do not refer to it as such so that their disciples, for their own protection, do not start dwelling upon it. It can be crossed only with the help of a spiritual Master. Hence, though there are six great spiritual regions, only five are named as such in Sant Mat literature, and this one is included in the five without mentioning it as a separate region. Therefore, Daswan Dwar is really Sunn and Maha Sunn combined.

Maharaj   Literally, great king; a title of respect.

mahatma   Great soul; also applied to highly spiritual persons.

Maha Yuga   See: Yuga.

Mahesh *or* **Maheshwar**   The same as Shiva.

Man (pronounced mun)   Mind.

manas   Mind; pertaining to the mind.

manmukh   Literally, facing the mind; one who obeys the dictates of the mind; a materialist or worldly person as opposed to a spiritual person. See also: gurmukh.

Mansur   A Muslim saint of Persia (870-923 A.D.).

Manu   An ancient lawgiver who divided Indian society into the four castes.

mardang   A musical instrument, resembling a long drum; also called mridang.

marg   Path or way.

mat   Creed; system; way; religion; teachings.

mauj   Literally, wave; will; especially the will and pleasure of the Sat Guru or the Supreme Being.

Mauj Puri   A place of Hindu pilgrimage.

Maulvi   A Muslim priest; one learned in Islamic religion and theology.

Maulvi Rum, Maulana Rum *or* **Rumi**   A well-known Muslim saint of Persia (1207-1277), who was a devoted disciple of Shamas-i-Tabriz; author of the world-famous *Masnavi*.

maya   Illusion or delusion; deception; unreality, phenomenal universe; all that is not eternal, is not real or true is called maya; it appears but is not. The veil of maya's illusion conceals the vision of God from our sight.

moh   Attachment; worldly attachments or entanglements; one of the five deadly passions (lust, anger, greed, attachment, ego). See also: kam, krodh, lobh, ahankar.

Mohammed   See: Hazrat Mohammed.

moksha   Salvation or liberation from the cycle of transmigration.

Mukam-i-Haq   Same as Sat Lok.

mul chakra   The rectal plexus.

mumuksha   One who desires to attain liberation (*moksha*).

Mundaka   The name of one of the Upanishads.

muni   A sage; holy man; one who contemplates.

murshid   Persian Islamic term for Master.

N

nabhi   Navel.

Nad   Sound; Shabd; Word; inner music.

Nad-bindu   The Sound out of which all things grow; the name of one of the Upanishads.

Nam *or* **Name**   Name; the Shabd, Logos, or Word; the divine creative power.

nam bhakti   Devotion to nam.

Nanak   See: Guru Nanak.

neel chakra *or* **nil chakra**   Blue centre, esoteric term for a certain stage in the ascent of the soul within.

newli karma *or* **neoli karma**   A yogic exercise of lowering the shoulders and flattening the back and, by the force of the breath, moving the abdomen right and left as well as up and down, as curds are churned in the churning vessel.

nij   Literally, means "one's own"; real; higher; innermost.

nij dham   One's own real home.

nijmanas   The inner mind, corresponding to causal body (*karan sharir*).

niranjan   Literally, means pure; an appellation of the Lord of the first spiritual region.

nirat   The soul's power of seeing; the attention inside.

nirguna   Without attributes; appellation for God. See also: guna.

nirvikalpa   Unwavering, concentrated; a state of deep meditation (*samadhi*) in which the disciple cannot distinguish himself from the object of meditation.

nuqta-i-swaida   Black point; third eye; Arabic name for *tisra til* or third eye.

nuri sarup   Light body; the Radiant Form of the Master; the astral form.

O

om   The sound symbol of Brahm; audible life stream or sound of the second spiritual region. See also: Shabd.

Ormuzd   The old Persian and Parsi term for God; an angel; also the planet Jupiter.

P

Padam Puran   A mythological book giving a detailed account of the cycles of the four yugas.

Paltu Sahib *or* **Paltoo Sahib** (1710–1780):   A famous Indian saint noted for his bold and clear description of the path of the Masters, which leads to the highest spiritual region.

Pandavas   The five Pandavas were the sons of Pandu, who was the brother of Dhrita-rashtra, King of Hastinapur. Dhrita-rashtra was blind, and Pandu died at a young age. The sons of Dhrita-rashtra were called the Kauravas. The Pandavas were deprived of their rightful inheritance, which was the cause of the great war between the Pandavas and the Kauravas, known as the Mahabharat.

pandit *or* **pundit**   One learned in Hindu theology and religion; the Hindu priestly class; Brahman priest; any Brahman.

par   Beyond.

Paramatma *or* **Parmatma**   The supreme soul or God. See also: Radha Soami.

param sant   A supreme saint; a saint who has attained the highest spiritual region.

Parbrahm   Beyond Brahm; the regions beyond Brahm Lok.

parmarth   Spiritual way of life; spiritual work; spiritual gain; spiritual effort; spiritual uplift.

parshad, parshadi, *or* **prasad**   Anything sanctified or blessed.

Patanjali   An ancient sage, known for his treatise on yoga.

pie   Smallest Indian coin, lowest in value, no longer in use.

Pind *or* **Pinda**   The physical universe; the physical body of man; the name of the lowest grand division of the creation. See also: Anda, Brahmand, Sach Khand.

pindi man   Physical (lower or material) aspect of the mind which governs the physical frame and senses.

pingala   See: sushumna.

prakriti   Nature; jyoti; maya; female energy or *shakti* of any deity; the essential nature of mind and matter, which projects itself in various forms of emotions and actions, and which also influences the various parts of the body; *prakritis* are twenty-five in number and consist of five principal manifestations of the five elements in the body.

prakritis   These are twenty-five in number and consist of five manifestations of each of the five elements or *tattwas*:

1. ether – Desires, anger, bashfulness, fear, infatuation.
2. air – Running, walking, smelling, contracting, expanding.
3. fire – Hunger, thirst, sleep, personality, laziness.
4. water – Vital fluid, blood, fat, urine, saliva.
5. earth – Bones, flesh, skin, veins, hair.

pralabdh *or* **prarabdh**   The fate karma; our destiny in this life, created by actions in past lives upon which the present life is based. See also: karma.

prana *or* **pran**   Vital force, essence or vital air.

pranayam   Part of the Patanjal yoga system, which attempts to control the vital air (*pran*), mainly through breath control. This practice is not recommended without an adept or Guru as a guide. See also: Guru.

prem marg   The path (*marg*) of love (*prem*); the path of the saints. Also called: bhakti marg.

purush   A being; creative energy; man.

Purusha and Prakriti region   The first spiritual region, where *prakriti* or *jyoti* has merged into Niranjan. *Purusha* and *prakriti* extend up to Brahm; then Brahm alone remains, up to Par Brahm.

Q

Quran *or* **Koran**   The holy book of the Muslims, revealed to Prophet Mohammed.

R

radha   Primal soul.

Radha Soami *or* **Radha Swami**   Lord (*soami*) of the soul (*radha*); appellation of the absolute Supreme Being.

Radha Soami Din Dayal   Literally, "Lord of the Soul, merciful to the humble."

Raheem, Rahim, *or* **Rahman**   Literally, "merciful", "forgiving"; used as a reference to God; Allah.

rajogun *or* **rajas**   The creative or active attribute (guna). See also: tamogun, satogun.

Raj Yoga   A practice that deals with the control of the currents of the mind by increasing the power of the mind through contemplation and certain postures. This practice is not recommended without an adept or Guru as guide.

Ram *or* **Rama**   A name for God; the power that pervades everything: a Hindu god.

Ramayana   The oldest of Sanskrit epic poems, written by the sage Valmiki. The Ramayana by Tulsi Das was written much later.

Ram Chandra   The same as Rama, king of Ayodhya, the seventh incarnation of the god Visnhu, believed to have lived in the Treta Yuga or second age. The story of his life is the subject of the Ramayana in Sanskrit by Valmiki.

Rehman   Same as Rahman.

rishi   One who sees, enlightened one; sage of ancient India, having some level of spiritual attainment, though usually not a saint. See also: sant, yogi.

roop   Form.

S

Sach Khand, Sat Desh, Sat Lok *or* **Nij Dham**   True or imperishable region, the name of the fifth spiritual region (Sat Lok) or the highest grand division of the creation. Region of the true Lord (Sat Purush, Sat Nam).

sadhu *or* **sadh**   One who has controlled the mind; technically, a devotee who has crossed the region of mind and matter and reached the third spiritual region (Daswan Dwar); sometimes applied to one who has gained the second region (Trikuti); generally, a holy man following a path of spiritual discipline.

sadhu seva   Rendering service to *sadhus*.

Sahansdal Kanwal, Sahans Dal Kamal, *or* **Sahasradal Kamal**   The thousand-petalled lotus, the name of the first spiritual region; the astral region.

sahib   Lord; honorable sir; a term of respect.

samadhan   Deep meditation, superconsciousness; a state of rapture.

samadhi   A state of concentration in which all consciousness of the outer world is transcended.

samhita   A code of laws, e.g., the Manu Samhita.

sannyasi   One who has renounced the world, who is free from attachments.

sannyasin   Feminine form of *sannyasi*.

sanskara   Impressions or tendencies from previous births, early upbringing, traditions and social influences, which shape the basic outlook and behavior patterns of a human being.

sanskari   One with a previous background; best fitted spiritually; predestined; a seeker after God.

sant   Saint; one who has attained the fifth spiritual region (Sach Khand); a God-realized soul. See also: Param Sant, Sant Mat.

Sant Mat   The teachings (*mat*) of the saints (*sant*). See also: Surat Shabd Yoga.

Sant Satguru   A saint who is also a spiritual teacher. Everyone who has reached the fifth spiritual region is a saint, but not all of them accept followers or are designated to teach. Hence, every true Master or Satguru is a saint, but not all saints are Satgurus.

sar   Essential; important; real; essence; true.

Sar Bachan   Literally, essential, true, or important words. The name of a book by Soami Ji.

Sar Shabd *or* **Sar Shabda**   The essence (*sar*) of the Word or Sound (*shabd*); the pure Shabd, free from matter, above Trikuti. See also: Anhad Shabd.

sat   True, real, everlasting. See also: Satguru, Sat Desh, Sat Lok, Sat Purush.

Sat Desh   True (*sat*) home or region (*desh*); another name for Sach Khand. See also: Sat Lok.

Satguru *or* **Satgur**   True (*sat*) spiritual teacher (*guru*); perfect Master; true light-giver; a Master who has access to the fifth spiritual region (Sach Khand). A *Satguru* teaches utmost humility, truth and compassion, earns his own living, and never charges for his teachings.

Satguru seva   Service to the Satguru; the real way to render him service, and that which he will always accept, is for the disciple to attend to meditation regularly.

Sat Lok   True (*sat*) region (*lok*); another name for Sach Khand. See also: Sat Desh.

Sat Nam   True (*sat*) Name (*nam*); the unspoken, unwritten Name or Word of God, the supreme Creator, lord of the fifth spiritual region, original source of souls; the true spiritual Father. See also: Sat Purush.

sato guna, satogun, *or* **satwa guna**   The quality or attribute of rhythm, harmony, and truth. See also Gunas.

Sat Purush   True or eternal (*sat*) being (*purush*); Supreme Being; God: lord of the fifth spiritual region. See also: Sat Nam.

satsang   True (*sat*) company (*sang*); association with the true; the company of or association with a perfect Master is external satsang; association of the soul with the Radiant Form of the Master, the Shabd or Nam within, is internal satsang. The highest form of satsang is to merge in the Shabd. A congregation assembled to hear a spiritual discourse is also referred to as satsang; even to think about the Master and his teachings is a form of satsang.

satsangi   One who associates with the true; initiate of a perfect Master; esoterically, one who has reached the first stage.

Sat Shabd   Literally, True Word; the Divine Sound.

Sat Yuga   True (*sat*) age (*yuga*), the Golden Age, the first of the four great cycles of time. See also: yuga.

Sawan   The chief rainy month in India, which corresponds with the latter part of July and the first two weeks of August.

Sawan Singh Ji Maharaj   Known as "the Great Master," he was the favourite and devoted disciple of Baba Jaimal Singh Ji in the Punjab. While Baba Jaimal Singh Ji was the one who first settled in and established what is known as the Radha Soami colony at Beas, it was Sawan Singh Ji Maharaj who actually built and developed it into the flourishing place which it now is. He attracted souls from all walks of life and from all corners of the world. He was born in village Jatana near Mehmansinghwalla, District Ludhiana (Punjab), his ancestral home, on July 19/20,[1] 1858, was appointed successor by Baba Jaimal Singh Ji Maharaj in 1903 and assiduously served in that capacity until his departure on 2 April, 1948.

seva *or* **sewa**   Service; voluntary service to the Master or his disciples. Of the four types of seva (monetary, physical, mental, spiritual), the highest form is the spiritual—the meditation practice.

Shabd *or* **Shabda**   Word or Sound; spiritual sound; audible life stream; sound current. The creative power, the source of all creation, which manifests as sound and light in the spiritual regions. It is the Word or Logos of the Bible; Kalma, Isme-i-Azam, Bang-i-Asmani, or Kalam-i-Ilahi of the Koran; the Nad of the Vedas; Nam, Ram Nam, Gurbani, Bani, and Dhun of the Adi

---

1. July 27th had previously been given as the birth date as that is the date on which it used to be celebrated at the Dera. The actual birth date was 5th Sawan 1915 Bikrami, according to the Indian Calendar, which corresponds to the 19th/ 20th July, 1858.

Granth; the Tao of the Chinese; Vadan; and the Saut-i-Surmad of the Sufis. The Zoroastrians call it Shraosha, and it is known by many other names. The secret of hearing the Shabd within oneself can be imparted only by a true Master (*Satguru*). See also: Shabd-dhun, Surat Shabd Yoga, Anhad Shabd.

shabds Hymns; paragraphs or stanzas of sacred texts put to music; often sung by a singer (*pathi*) accompanying a discourse at satsang. These are external sounds, as opposed to inner Sound (*Shabd*). See also: Shabd, satsang.

Shabd Yog Same as Surat Shabd Yog.

Shabd-dhun Music (*Dhun*) of the Word (*shabd*); the Shabd; the audible life stream.

Shabd marg The path (*marg*) of the Word (*shabd*); the path of Shabd Yoga, the path of the saints. See also: Surat Shabd Yoga.

Shah Rag *or* **Shah Rug** Literally, "royal vein," but this does not refer to a vein in the physical body. It is the central current or canal in the finer body, which is located and traversed by means of spiritual practice according to the instructions of a true Master. It is the same as *sushmana* or *sushmuna*, which is the central current. The current on the left is called *ida* or *ira*, and that on the right is known as *pingala*.

shakti Power, ability or strength; the highest form of *maya*, or illusion.

Shamas-i-Tabriz *or* **Shams-i-Tabriz (1206-1248):** Shams-Uddin Mohammed Tabriz, better known as Shams-i-Tabriz, a famous Muslim Saint of Persia, was born in Tabriz, Iran. He was the Master of Maulana Rum who named his composition after the name of his Master—Diwan-i-Shams-Tabriz. He was assassinated by religious fanatics.

Shankaracharya A great commentator of the Vedanta Sutras and the Upanishads.

shanti Peace; peace of mind.

shariat Islamic code of life, religious law, justice; Koranic law and ritual.

Shastras Hindu scriptures; books of philosophy and moral code.

Shiva   God of destruction in the Hindu trinity of creator, preserver, destroyer (Brahma, Vishnu, Shiva).

shraddha   Faith, belief, reverence.

Shraosha   Zarathrustra used the term to refer to the inner Sound, the Shabd. It is referred to as the most majestic aspect or power of Ahura Mazda because it brings eternal life.

sikh *or* **shiskya**   Literally, disciple or follower; the same as chela; the followers of Guru Nanak and his nine successors are known as Sikhs. The name also applies to one who has reached the first spiritualregion within.

sikhi   The path of discipleship.

simran *or* **sumiran**   Repetition or loving remembrance; repetition of the five holy names according to the instructions of a perfect Master. The simran that a perfect Master gives is charged with his power; disciples concentrate the attention at the third eye (*tisra til*) and carry on repetition with love and one-pointed attention. This practice enables them to withdraw the soul currents from the body to the third eye, from where the real spiritual journey begins.

sinchit *or* **sanchit**   The store of unpaid past karmas. It is from this store that the fate karmas (*pralabdh*) are drawn. See also: karma.

Soami *or* **Swami**   Lord; the Supreme Being; the Master; commonly applied to all spiritual teachers. See also: Radha Soami.

Soami Ji *or* **Swami Ji (1818-1878):**   The Great Saint and founder of what is now known as the Radha Soami faith, science and philosophy. His real name was Seth Shiv Dayal Singh. See Radha Soami Dayal.

Sufi   An adherent of Sufism, which is a mystic sect developed in Persia, who believe in a living Murshid (Guru) and lead a holy life. The term is now being used to denote any holy man among the Muslims.

Sukshm Sarup   Subtle form; astral body.

Sukshm Shahrir   Same as Sukshm Sarup.

Sultan-ul-Azkar   Literally, the king of methods. A reference to the Surat Shabd yoga.

Sumeru   Another name for Mount Meru, the place where gods are said to reside; symbolically, the top of the spine. It is also called the Golden Mountain, Jewel Park, Lotus Mountain, and Mountain of the gods.

Sunn *or* **Sunna**   Derived from Sanskrit *shunya*, it has usually been translated as void, emptiness, vacuum; but the saints have not used this term in this meaning. According to them it is an inner spiritual region which is devoid of matter in any form. On entering this region the soul becomes free from the bondage of matter, mind and the three attributes.

Surat   Soul; consciousness; inner attention. As consciousness in the body is due to the presence of the soul, hence the soul is also called *surat*.

Surat Shabd Yoga   The practice of joining the soul (*surat*) with the Word (*shabd*) and merging (*yoga*) with it; once the soul merges into the Shabd, it is carried by the Shabd to its source, the Lord.

sushumna *or* **sushmana**   The central current in the finer body, starting from the eye centre and leading upward to the higher spiritual regions, located and traversed by means of the spiritual practice taught by a perfect Master; also known as *Shah Rag*. It is not to be confused with *sushumna* of the yogis, which is the central canal along the spine in the lower body and is to be ignored by satsangis and spiritual practitioners. The *sushumna* divides into two currents, on the left is *ida* and on the right is *pingala*.

swarath   Worldly duties; worldly work; selfishness.

Swarg, Swarga, *or* **Swarg Lok**   Heaven or Paradise in general; the same as Bahisht and Baikunth.

T

tama, tamo-guna, *or* **tamogun**   The attribute of dissolution, inertia, darkness. See also: guna, satogun, rajogun.

Tathagata   One who has attained; a name for the Buddha.

tattwa   Elements, essence; the five elements are present, to various degrees, in all living beings: earth (*prithvi*), water (*jal*), fire (*agni*), air (*vayu*), and ether (*akash*).

til   Literally, seed of the sesamum plant; esoterically, the small aperture through which the soul enters Brahmand from Pind; the centre between the eyebrows.

tisra til   Third (*tisra*) eye (*til*); a point in the subtle body, between and behind the two eyebrows; the seat of the mind and the soul in the human body, and the point at which the disciples of the saints begin their concentration, and from where they go up. Also called 'the "black point" (*nuqta-i-saveida*) by Sufis and 'the "single eye" in the Bible.

titiksha   Endurance, patience; power of enduring hardships with calmness and peace.

Treta Yuga   The Silver Age, the second grand cycle of time, immediately following the Golden Age (Sat Yuga). See also: yuga.

Trikuti   Three prominences; that part of the subtle universe which lies above the astral world; the name of the second spiritual region; the causal region. Also called: Brahm Lok.

Triloki   Three worlds: the physical world (Pind), astral world (Anda) and the causal world (Brahmand), all ruled by Brahm.

Tulsi Das   A Saint of medieval times, author of the Ramayana in Hindi.

Tulsi Sahib   A great poet-saint of Hathras, and exponent of Sant Mat and the author of *Ghat Ramayana*. He was born in the princely family of Peshwas in 1763 and was heir to the throne of the kingdom of Poona and Sitara. He began to show signs of a devotional trend of mind at a very early age, and had no attachments or desires for worldly pleasures and pursuits. A few days before his coronation was to take place, he left his home and fled towards the North in the garb of a sadhu. He settled in Hathras, near Aligarh, in the U.P., where he was known as Dakkhini Baba (the Sage from the South). Soami Ji's mother was a disciple of Tulsi Sahib long before Soami Ji was born, and Soami Ji himself received Light from him. Tulsi Sahib departed from this world in 1848.

Turiya Pad   Another name for Sahansdal Kanwal. The state of superconsciousness where the soul makes its first contact with the real Shabd.

U

Upanishads   The philosophical and mystical part of the Vedas relating to esoteric teachings. Upanishad literally means "to sit near or close," and the doctrines were so named because these secrets and mysteries were personally imparted to the disciple by the teacher.

uparati   Renunciation; detachment from all worldly desires.

V

Vah Guru *or* **Wahi Guru**   The Sikh name for God; the Supreme Lord.

vairagya   Detachment, particularly mental detachment from the world and worldly desires; a state of mind—not to be confused with asceticism or physical renunciation of the world.

vairagi   One who has attained detachment.

varnatmak   Describable; that which can be spoken or written. See also: dhunatmak.

Vedant *or* **Vedanta**   A system of Indian philosophy, based particularly on the Upanishads, believing in the unitary existence of God and the identity of the soul with God.

Vedantic   Pertaining to Vendanta.

Vedas   Literally, knowledge; revealed as embodied in the four holy books of the Hindus: Rig Veda, Sam Veda, Yajur Veda and Atharva Veda.

Vedic   Pertaining to the Vedas.

vina, veena *or* **beena, bina**   A stringed musical instrument, perhaps the oldest of the classical musical instruments in India, said to be the forerunner of the sitar. While *vina* is the correct name for this stringed instrument referred to in Sant Mat literature, some authors have used the term *bin* or *been*, which should not be confused with the Scottish bagpipe. The exact

sound of the region of Sach Khand cannot be conveyed in terms
of any material musical instrument, as nothing in this world
comes anywhere near that divine melody. In fact, like the light
of that region, its sound also defies terrestrial comparison.

Vishnu   God of preservation in the Hindu trinity of creator, preserver, destroyer (Brahma, Vishnu, Shiva).

vivek   Discrimination; searching inquiry, careful study, as the first
step on the path of the Masters.

W

Wahiguru   Same as Vah Guru.

wheel of   See: chaurasi.

Y

yag, yagya, *or* **yajna**   Sacrifice, a ritual or religious ceremony, which
in ancient times often included the sacrifice of some animal.

Yama   The lord of death, who takes charge of the uninitiated soul
at the time of death. See also: yamdoot.

yamdoot   Messengers or angels (*doot*) of death (*yama*).

yoga   Literally, union; esoterically, spiritual exercises; practice;
meditation in the spiritual sense; any system which leads to or
aims at the union of the soul with God.

yogeshwar   King of yogis, or supreme yogi; one who has reached
the second spiritual region, Brahm Lok, the causal plane.

yogi   One who practices yoga.

yuga   Age; a great cycle of time. Hindu mythology divides time
into four recurring cycles: the Golden Age (Sat Yuga); the Silver
Age (Treta Yuga); the Copper Age (Dwapar Yuga); and the Iron
Age (Kal Yuga), through which we are now passing. One thousand yugas make a Great Age (Maha Yuga), which is equivalent
to one day of Brahm. Saints have adopted this concept to con-
vey the ever-changing nature of life on earth.

INDEX AND CONCORDANCE

A

A time for everything, 138.
Aberration, 172.
'*Abhyas*', 189.
Abode of the Supreme Father, 69.
Above all, do not miss your Bhajan and Simran every day, 143.
Abrasions, 84.
Absolute 'must' for ending the rounds of birth and death, 105.
    "   Reality, 111.
Accelerators, 174.
Account of 'Karmas' must be rendered (see also debt), 125, 183.
Accounts go with the soul wherever it is reborn, 97, 197.
Achieve purpose by, 195.
Acid test, 164, 172.
Act in such a way as to rise above them, 176.
Action and reaction (see also 'karma'), 79.
Actions of a devotee are opposite to the ways of the world, 199.
    "   speak louder than words, 181.
Actors, 106.
Adept, 69, 76, 78, 96, 101.
Advanced Satsangi can but does not misuse spiritual powers, 199.
Adverse or easy circumstances, 131.
Advice given by our Great Master, 137.
    "   of friends, 118.
    "   re. inner experiences, 174.
    "   re. meditation, 151, 164, 169, 170, 172, 178.
    "   to one who had recently retired on pension, 187.
    "   to Satsangi who had daily Darshan within and complained because he lost it, 191.
Advice to Satsangi whose non-Satsangi mother was ill, 170.
    "   to worried mother whose son was flying abroad, 196-197.
Aeroplanes, 10.

Affliction (see also disease, pain, poverty, suffering), 107.
After death, 13, 14, 39, 107.
Agam, 23.
Agent of Brahm, Kal, 99.
Agony, 60, 71, 77, 107, 197.
'*Ahimsa*' (see harmlessness).
Aids to the process of concentration, 141, 158-159.
Ailments, 14.
Aim (see also goal, object, purpose), 37, 38.
    "   and ambition of every disciple should be to, 157.
    "   of initiation, 138.
    "   should always be to, 159, 164.
Air, 31, 78.
'Akash', 31, 78.
'*Akash Bani*', 12.
'*Alakh*', 23.
Alcoholic drinks, 158.
Alexander the Great discovered the priceless value of a single breath too late and departed empty-handed, 192.
Alien country, land, 20, 78.
All disciples are not alike, 131.
" effort should be directed toward, 165.
" have the same origin, 111.
" human beings are one in Shabd, 126.
" people do not realize the purpose of life, 140.
" pervading, 165.
" things come to him who does his duty and, 139.
All thought and energy should be directed toward the eye centre, 157.
All Saints preached and followed this way, 82.
Allah, 5.
Almighty Father, 62.
Alone, 169.
Also a way to face and work off karmas, 176.
Altar of devotion, 92.
Altar of love, 183.
Always keep your mind in Simran, 188.

" keep your tongue under control, 185.

" reflect calmly, 189.

" remain under His protection, 185.

" speak kindly, 182.

Ambition, s, 157.

Ambrosia, 12.

America, 127.

Amount of time to devote to Spiritual exercises daily, 134, 136, 145, 160.

Amrit, 12, 19.

Amritsar, 200.

'Ana-ul-Haq', 23.

'Anahad Marg ', 10.

'Anahat', 11.

'Anahat Shabd', 19.

Analyze, 175.

'Anda', 29.

Anecdotes (see Illustrations, Examples, Quotations, Similes).

Angel, s, 6, 63, 91, 186.

Angels defined, 90-91.

Angles of death, 89.

Anger, 20, 163.

" burns up all that is noble, 71-72.

" consumes and destroys, 72.

" damages your liver and heart, and poisons your blood, 189.

Anguish, 71.

'Anhad', 11.

'Anhad Shabd', 34, 75, 80.

Animal food (flesh and eggs), 158, 163.

Animal killing, 60.

Animals, 6, 60, 63, 72, 73.

Animals have four active tattwas, 73.

Answers to some questions, 165.

Ant (first rate of speed of the soul), 133, 154.

Antagonism in Nam and Kam, 192.

Antagonistic to the Radha Soami Path, 134.

Antidote for all ills, 108.

Antidote for lack of devotion, 103.

'Anubhav', 45.

Aperture through which we pass beyond matter and mind, 82.

Apertures (see also Nine doors, Gates, outlets), 49.

Appalling conditions, 89.

Apparent contradiction, 97.

Apparent lack of progress, 154.

Applicants, 157, 158.

Appreciation of the Master's help, 147.

Apprehension, 103.

'Apregreha' (see Negation of desire).

Arab, 7.

Ardour, 131.

Argument, s 129, 144, 176.

Arjan Dev (see Guru Arjan Dev).

Arms, 170.

Arrangements, for reaching Sach Khand go on side by side with the disciple's Fate Karma, 167.

'Arti', 98.

Artificial and dangerous method, 140.

'Asanas', 10.

Ascension (see Progressive stages of the soul, Withdrawal, Rise above the nine portals of the body).

'Asht Dal Kanwal', 19.

'Ashtang Yoga', 46.

'Ashtangi', 31.

Aspirin, 119.

Assert your will (to dismiss all irrelevant thoughts), 161.

'Astaiya' (see Stealing prohibited).

Astral body, 58.

" form of the Master (see also Radiant Form, Inner Master), 99.

" form of the Master is met after crossing the inner solar system, 155.

Astral form of the Master is Radiant, Beautiful and Magnetic, 193.

" region. 58.

'At attention', spiritually, 182.

'At will', 155.

Atonement (see Account, Debt, Payment Vicarious Atonement).

Attach yourself, your soul, to the True Eternal Word, Sound Current, 13, 71, 85.

Attachment or infatuation is the most insidious and deceitful of the passions, 72.

Attachment seduces and procrastinates, 72.

Attachments in life are unreal, 106.

Attack the mind with full force, 188.

Attend to Bhajan and Simran, 191.

" to no sound, not even the bell sound, when it emanates from the left, 137.

" to your work during the day, 84.

Attention has been 'out' for ages, to draw it 'in' requires time and effort, 154.

Attention has been scattered outside, 14.

Attention has to be withdrawn from the body and concentrated at the eye centre, 155.

Attention is to do the Simran, 189.

Attention should be concentrated, 16, 68, 75.

Attention should be fixed while repeating, 170.

Attitude, s, 160, 171, 176, 202.

Attitude of concealing one's Master often arises from, 127.

Attitude of good and loving feelings towards others, 150.

Attitude of humility should be adopted, 182.

Attractive, 118.

Attune yourself to the Voice of the Lord, 13.

Audible Life Stream is inside and can be heard by anyone who, 164.

Audible Life Stream, The (see also Nam, Shabd, Sound Current, Word), 11, 53, 80, 163.

Audibly, 148.

Austerities, 18, 46, 76.

Austerities do not take us beyond the six centres, 82.

Automobile, 10.

Avail of this gift, 201.

Avarice (see also Greed), 20.

Avarice binds us to material things and clouds our vision, 71, 72.

'Avidya' (see also Shakti), 33.

Avoid mistakes in future, 176.

Avoid over-indulgence, 151.

Avoid pitfalls and temptations, 53.

Avoid the life of sensual pleasures, 193.

Awaken dormant faculties, 163.

Awaken your love for the Supreme Being, 13.

Awe, 54.

Axiom, 77.

B

'Baang', 12.

Baba Jaimal Singh Ji Maharaj, 177.

Baba Ji (same as Baba Jaimal Singh Ji Maharaj).

Baba Sawan Singh Ji (see Maharaj Baba Sawan Singh Ji). 53.

Baba Tal, the young son of Guru Hargobind Ji, 199-200.

Baby, 198.

Back to Nature, 128.

Bad actions, 53.

Bad bargain, 80.

Bad (Rajasik or Tamasik) food, 187.

Bald-headed person who was blind and deaf, 74.

Balloon, 118.

'Bani' (see also Teachings, Nam, Shabd, Sound Current, Word), 12, 80, 177.

Bankruptcy, 103.

Baptism and various sacraments, 18.

Bar to spiritual progress, 109.

Barriers which stand in the way of crossing the boundary of Brahm, 125.

Barring the way to God-Realization, 196.

Baseless pursuits, 89.

Basic perspective, 194.

Basic principle, 14.

Baths in 'holy waters', 17, 46.

Battle between mind and soul, 188.

Be firm and steadfast, 172.

Be steadfast in your meditation, 183.

Beads, counting or telling of, 7, 76.

Beas river, 192.

Beast kills to satisfy hunger, but man does it for pleasure, 78.

Beast of burden, 181.

Beasts, 63.

Become one with it (Shabd), 68.

Beauties of Nature, 84.

Before beginning meditation, 169.

Before birth, 89.

Before meditation period, 146.

Beginner, 131, 132, 133, 134, 147, 153, 154, 155, 156.

Beginning is dry and tedious, 156.

Beginning is slow and laborious, 153.

Behaviour (see also Attitude, Conduct), 134, 190, 193.

Behold radiant light within, 76.

Behold the beauties of Nature, 84.

'Bekh', defined, 4.

Bell sound, 20.

Benevolence, 147.

Bereaved, Bereavement (see also Death, Grief), 71, 78.

Bride's, 108.

Bridle, 149.

Brief delirium of power, 104.

Brilliant white light surrounded by twinkling lights, 174.

Bundle of filth, 75.

'Bunk Nal,' 21.

Burden of your *Karma* is being lightened day by day, 133.

Business, 8, 145.

Business advice, 133.

Business ups and downs, 146.

Butcher Saint, 73.

Butchering (see killing).

By and by it will be complete, 176.

C

Calmly and gently, 173, 189.

Camel, 201.

Career, 145.

Cares, 151.

Cart before the horse, 148.

Caste, 64.

Catastrophe, 78.

Catastrophic happenings, 178.

Cattle, 105.

Causal body, mind, 57-58, 166.

Causal region, 58, 166.

Cause of feeling of distress and depression, 19.

Cause of our troubles in this life, 144.

Cause of recurring woe and misery, 65.

Cave, 22, 27.

Celestical Flame, 68.

Celestical Sound, Music, 48, 80.

Celibate, 10.

Cemeteries, 71.

Centre from which all thoughts and energy go out, 9.

Center of consciousness (see also Third Eye), 9, 162-163.

Centre where *Nam* reverberates constantly, 93.

Centres, plexuses, lotuses or Kanwals, *chakras* or ganglia in the body, 6, 30, 34.

Ceremonies, 39, 64.

Chain of action and reaction, 62.

Chain, s, of bondage, 14, 53, 78, 98.

Chain of desires that brings us back to this world, 104.

Chain of Infinite Love, 101.

Chains that tie the soul to this world, 98.

Chakras, lotuses, *kanwals,* centres, plexuses or ganglia, 6, 8-9.

Chakras, detailed description of, 30-33.

Change, changed conditions, 136, 144.

Change is written large on everything, everywhere, 104.

Character, 188, 192.

Characteristic of the mind, 161.

Characteristic of this world, 137.

Charcoal, 38-39.

Charitable view, 131.

Charities, 46, 81.

Chasing a mirage, 93.

Chasteners, 201.

Chastening and purifying influence on the mind, 146.

Chastity, 32, 95, 190, 208.

'Chaurasi', 52.

Cheerful, 169.

'Chitakash', 32.

Child, 46, 54, 168.

Childhood, 91.

Children, 14, 52, 136, 193.

Choice of the seeker, 53.

Chosen of God, 94.

Christ (see also Quotations), 63, 74, 80, 166, 201.

Christ called it WORD, 163.

Christians, 18, 41.

Church, es, 81, 130.

Churning water and churning milk, 75.

Circumstances in life depend upon past *karma,* 131.

Clansman, 12.

Cleanliness, 190.

Clear thinking is ninety per cent *'Abhyas',* 189,

Climb up, 69.

Close the nine doors, 75, 195.

Cockpit, 137.

Cold logic, 144.

Colour, 64.

Colours of tattwas, 30.

Colt, 149.

Come Home, 94.

Come to the Realm of the Master, 69.

Comfort, 143, 148.

Command as embodied in the Last Will

H

Tulsi Das, 43, 44.
Quran, 5, 11.

R

Race, 64.
Radha Swami, 23, 24.
"   "   disciples, 137.
"   "   does not impose this diet for
             the sake of form, 144-145.
"   "   Faith becoming prevalent in
             your country, all depends
             on, 146.
"   "   Faith does not impose
             dogmatic beliefs, 161.
"   "   Followers should have a
             stronger mind than to, 144-
             145.
"   "   *Pad,* 23, 24.
"   "   *Path,* 130, 134.
"   "   prescribes a method of
             practice by which conce-
             ntration can be brought
             about 'at will', 155.
"   "   students may associate with
             students travelling other
             spiritual paths, 175-176.
Radiant Form of the Master within, 191.
"   *Shabd* Form, 117.
Radio, 146.
Rajas defined, 94.
Rajasic food, 187-188.
Ram, Rama, 12, 43.
Ram Dhum 12.
Ramayana, 43.
Rare gifts, 201-202.
"   privilege, 52.
Ravana king of Lanka, 181.
Reaction, 160-161.
"   of sense enjoyment, 79.
Read all the available literature on this
      Path, 140.
Real from *Sant Mat* literature twice daily,
      198, 199.
Reading good books, 138, 139.
"   Study of Scriptures, 17, 18, 46.
Read appreciation comes when, 147.
"   chanting, 105, 106, 107.
"   feet of the Master are within you,
      157.
Real form of the Master is *Shabd,* 122.
"   Home, 14, 15, 37, 38 , 61, 62.

"   knowledge, 91, 92.
"   method of overcoming sexual
             desires, 152, 153.
"   *Nam,* dispensed only by, 177, 178.
"   *Nam* is *Shabd,* 46.
"   problem, *the* problem, 118.
"   renunciation, 169, 170.
"   seekers after Truth are very few, 123.
"   spiritual progress begins after, 160.
"   teaching of Christ, 166.
"   vs. shadow or reflection, 6, 7, 34.
"   work, 85.
Reality, 100-101.
Realization beyond the three worlds comes
      only when *Nam* or *Shabd* is contacted
      by the soul, 91-92.
"   of God is Bliss, 100, 101, 102.
Reapers, 89.
Reaping and sowing, 99, 150, 151.
Reason (reasoning), 176, 177.
Reason defined, 195-196.
"   for your inability to go in, 135.
Reasoning and self-control, 157-158.
"   takes us only to a certain point, 45.
Reborn in the form in which we can best
      fulfil our desires, 15.
Recapitulation, 15, 24, 40, 54, 76.
Rechak, 33.
Recitation, 17, 18.
Recrudescence of the trouble, 175-176.
Rectal centre (*Mul Chakra*), 8.
Redeemer, 178.
Reflections of the real, 6, 33, 34.
Regard worldly possessions as a loan,
      105,106.
Regular, one-pointed *Simran,* 161.
Regularity of (practice) essential, 118, 119,
             135, 140, 142, 147, 149, 160, 161,
             178, 197.
Reincarnation and cause of rebirth, 97.
Relation of husband and wife, 132.
Relations and family members, 132.
Relationship of the devotee, the Satguru
      and God, 101.
Relationships on material plane are all
      based on selfish motives, 132.
Relatives, 12, 13.
Relative, positions of various stages and
      regions along the Path, 36, 37, 38.
Relax, ation, 174-175.
Release from the prison-house, bondage,

circumstances, 143.
" duty 159.
" exercises, 85, 136.
" fragrance, 192.
" healing, 207.
" heritage, 165.
" journey, 7.
" journey (withdrawal) begins from the toes and ends at the top of the head, 121, 122, 148, 149, 153.
" journey is divided into two parts, 121, 122, 153, 162.
Spiritual Path, 119, 120.
" poverty, 194.
" powers not to be used toward worldly ends, 199-200, 207-208.
" practice, 19.
" practice, regularly, without fail, 178.
" progress is to be judged by, 150-151.
" progress makes one indifferent to worldly surroundings, 155.
" progress of individual is also helpful to others, 123.
" research, 95.
" School, 130.
" structure is behind the curtain of the mind, 162-163.
Spiritualism, 134.
Spiritually asleep, 112.
" speaking, 117.
Spot which represents the end of one course and the beginning of another, 119-120.
Squabbles of the world, 124-125.
Stages of ascent of the soul, 19-24.
" of descent of the soul, 67-68.
Stand 'at attention', spiritually, 182.
Steadfastly, steadfastness, 133-134, 182.
Steadiness and perseverance, 158.
Stealing or desiring to do so is prohibited, 190.
Stilling the mind is achieved only by degrees, 149.
Stored impressions, 149.
Storehouse of *Pranas,* 31-32.
Storm the dark fortress of *Kal* and *Krmas,* 194-195.
Straight road that takes us back to our True Spiritual Home, 162-163.
Strain, 130-131, 140, 148, 157, 174, 175.

" comes where the mind is involved, Stranger, 89, 108.
Strict code of discipline, 190.
Strife, 149.
Strive, but without being affected by the results, 143.
Strong will power is developed by *Simran alone,* 188.
Struggle between matter and consciousness," is characteristic of this world, 137.
" will be won when, 134.
Students travelling other spiritual paths, 175-176.
Study of religious books, 190.
Subconscious repetition of Names, 175.
Subdue the mind, 187-204.
Substances of animal origin, (see also Diet, Food), 119.
Subtle mind, 68.
Success may not always be apparent to you, 161.
" will one day be yours, 154.
Succor, 198.
Suction, 174.
Suffering, 58, 65, 66, 71, 76, 97, 103, 149.
Suicide, 13, 14, 189.
" greatest of all sins, 197-198.
Sultan-al-Azkar (King of Methods) 10.
Superconscious energy, 65.
" within 112, 159.
Superiority of man, (see also Value of Human form) 201.
Supermen, 145.
Supernatural powers, 30, 53, 199-200.
Support and Sustenance of all, 46.
Supreme Being, Lord, is within us, 12, 32.
" creator, 109.
" Father, 69.
Surat Shabd Yoga, 10, 16, 40.
" " " is not a new science, 82, 108.
Sure sign that the soul is on its way up, 69.
Surgeons, 10, 112.
Surrender to God, complete, 190.
" to Him completely, 198.
" to the Will of the Master, 92, 100, 101, 177, 205.
" yourself to *Nam* or Word, 160-161.
Sushmana, 32, 82.
Sustainer, 5.

X

unknown factor, 126.

Y

Yag (see Sacrifices).
Yam, 190.
Yardstick of reason, 196.
Yearning for the Lord is the primary pre-
    requisite, 91-92.
   " must be sincere and true, 198.
   " to meet the Lord, 184.
'*Yog Shastra*' 190.
Yoga of Pranayam does not take us beyond
    the six centres, 82.
Yoga postures, positions, 159.
Yogic methods, 9.
Yogis, 89, 21.
   " are no doubt sincere but, 140.
Yogishwars, 24.
You can always write here for information,
    173.
   " can find intense light and numberless
    planes where unceasing music is
    going on, 164.
   " cannot deceive or defraud the Lord,
    183-184.
   " cannot go out and go in at the same
    time, 118-119.
   " cannot hustle the power within, 175.
You deceive no one but yourself, 184.

   " may refer your difficulties to me,
    160.
   " may write to me freely about your
    progress as well as your difficulties,
    141.
   " need not try to find the focus, 175.
   " should not be anxious about other
    seekers, 140.
   " should not expect result to soon 147.
   " will begin to rise above
    circumstances when, 148-149.
   " will get full advantage from the
    Sound Current when, 158-159.
   " will never be unhappy, is, 189.
   " will see and hear many, many things,
    136.
Young and old, 65.
Young widow, 185, 197.
Your desire for overindulgence will
    automatically vanish if, 144.
   " fort is your Guru, 185.
   " own work is *Simran* and *Bhajan,*
    85.
Youth, 89, 191.

Z

Zeal of most disciples is liable to cool
    down because, 131.

Addresses for Information and Books

INDIAN SUB-CONTINENT

INDIA
The Secretary
Radha Soami Satsang Beas
P.O. Dera Baba Jaimal Singh 143204
District Amritsar, Punjab

NEPAL
Mr. Dal Bahadur Shreshta
Radha Soami Satsang Beas
P. O. Box 1646, Gongabu, Dhapasi
Kathmandu

PAKISTAN
Mr. Dileep Kumar
18 B Lalazar, New Queens Road
Karachi, Sindh

SRI LANKA
Mr. Chandroo Mirpuri
39/3 Horton Palce
Colombo 7

SOUTHEAST ASIA

FOR FAR EAST
Mrs. Cami Moss
RSSB-HK
T.S.T. , P.O. Box 90745
Kowloon, Hong Kong

MALAYSIA
Mr. Selvarajoo Pragasam
No. 15 Jalan SL 10/4
Bandar Sg. Long
43000 Kajang

THAILAND
Mr. Harmahinder Singh Sethi
58/32 Rachdapitsek Road, Soi 16
Thapra, Bangkok Yai 10600

INDONESIA
Mr. Ramesh Sadarangani
Jalan Pasir Putih IV/16, Block E 4
Ancol Timur, Jakarta Utara 14430

PHILIPPINES
Mr. Kay Sham
Science of the Soul Study Center
Don Jesus Boulevard
Alabang Hills, Cupang 1771
Muntinlupa City, Metro Manila

SINGAPORE
Mrs. Asha Melwani
Radha Soami Satsang Beas Singapore
19 Amber Road, Singapore 439868

ASIA PACIFIC

AUSTRALIA
Mr. Pradeep Raniga
P.O. Box 642
Balwyn North, Victoria 3104

NEW ZEALAND
Mr. Tony Waddicor
Science of the Soul Study Centre
P. O. Box 5331
Auckland

GUAM
Mrs. Hoori M. Sadhwani
115 Alupang Cove
241 Condo Lane, Tamuning 96911

HONG KONG
Mr. Manoj Sabnani
RSSB-HK, 3rd Floor, Eader Centre
39-41 Hankow Road,
Tsim Sha Tsui, Kowloon

JAPAN
Mr. Jani G. Mohinani
Radha Soami Satsang Beas
1-2-18 Nakajimadori
Aotani, Chuo-Ku
Kobe 651-0052

SOUTH KOREA,
TAIWAN, R.O.C.
Mr. Haresh Buxani
3rd floor, Eader Centre
39-41 Hankow Road
Tsim Sha Tsui
Kowloon, Hong Kong

NORTH AMERICA

CANADA
Mr. John Abel
#701-1012 Beach Avenue
Vancouver, B.C. V6E 1T7

Mrs. Meena Khanna
149 Elton Park Road
Oakville, Ontario L6J 4C2

MEXICO
Dr. Hector Esponda
RSSB-Mexico
Circuito Universidad 360
(In front of Vista Vallarta Golf Club)
Puerto Vallarta, Jalisco 48290

UNITED STATES
Dr. Vincent P. Savarese
2550 Pequeno Circle
Palm Springs, CA 92264

Science of the Soul Study Center
2415 East Washington Street
Petaluma, CA 94954

Dr. Frank E. Vogel
71 Old Farm Road
Concord, MA 01742

Science of the Soul Study Center
4115 Gillespie Street
Fayetteville, NC 28306-9053

Dr. John Templer
114 Verdier Road
Beaufort, SC 29902-5440

Mr. Hank Muller
1900 North Loop West, Suite 500
Houston, TX 77018

ffffffffffffff4444ff4fff4

444fff44f4f4ff4

CARIBBEAN

FOR CARIBBEAN
Mr. Sean Finnigan
P. O. Box 2314
Port-au-Prince
Haiti, W. I.

BARBADOS
Mr. Deepak Nebhani
Radha Soami Satsang Beas
Lot No. 10, 5th Avenue
Belleville, St. Michael
Barbados, W. I.

CURACAO
Mr. Frank Claessen
La Quinta Villas 121
St. Catharina
Curacao, N.A.

GUYANA
Mrs. Rajni B. Manglani
A-80 Eping Avenue,
Bel Air Park,
Georgetown, Guyana

JAMAICA
Mrs. Shammi Khiani
P. O. Box 22
Montego Bay
Jamaica, W. I.

ST. MAARTEN
Mrs. Kanchan Mahbubani
R.S.S.B. Foundation
P. O. Box 978
Phillipsburg
St. Maarten, N. A.

SURINAME
Mr. Chandru Samtani
15 Venus Straat
Paramaribo
Suriname

TRINIDAD
Mr. Chandru Chatlani
20 Admiral Court
Westmoorings-by-Sea
Westmoorings
Trinidad, W.I.

CENTRAL AMERICA

BELIZE
Mrs. Chand Babani
5789 Goldson Avenue, Belize City

PANAMA
Mr. Deepak Dhanani
Altos Del Bosque
Residencial El Doral, Casa 195
Republica De Panama

SOUTH AMERICA

FOR SOUTH AMERICA
Mr. Hiro W. Balani
P.O. Box 486,
Malaga 29012, Spain

ARGENTINA
Mrs. Fabiana Shilton
Leiva 4363
Post Code 1427 Buenos Aires

BRAZIL
Mr. Willefort Leao
Rua Plinio Moscoso 1248
Edif. Sol de Verao, Apt. 201
40155-190, Salvador

CHILE
Mr. Vijay Harjani
Cosmos International S. A.
Manzana 5, Sitio 3
Iquique

COLOMBIA
Mrs. Emma Orozco
Calle 45, #99-25, Medellin

ECUADOR
Dr. Fernando Flores Villalva
Radha Soami Satsang Beas-Ecuador
Calle Marquez de Varela
Oe 3-68y Ave. America
P.O. Box 17-21-115, Quito

PERU
Mr. Carlos Fitts Villalva
P.O. Box 180658
Rinconada del Lago
1016-201 Lima

VENEZUELA
Mr. Jose Penaherrera
Calle "A", Residencias
Minarete, 9° Piso, Apto
91B, Urb.La Alameda,
Stafe, Caracas 1080

EUROPE

AUSTRIA
Mr. Hansjorg Hammerer
Sezenweingasse 10, Salzburg A-5020

BELGIUM
Mr. Piet J. E. Vosters
Driezenstraat 26
Turnhout 2300

BULGARIA
Mr. Emilio Saev
Foundation Radha Soami Satsang Beas
Bulgaria
P. O. Box 39, 8000 Bourgas

CYPRUS
Mr. Heraclis Achilleos
P. O. Box 29077, Nicosia 1035

CZECH REPUBLIC
Mr. Vladimir Skalsky
Maratkova 916,
420 00 Prague 411

DENMARK
Mr. Tony Sharma
Sven Dalsgaardsvej 33
DK-7430 Ikast

FINLAND
Ms. Anneli Wingfield
P. O. Box 1422
00101 Helsinki

FRANCE
Ct. Pierre de Proyart
7 Quai Voltaire,
Paris 75007

GERMANY
Mr. Rudolf Walberg
P. O. Box 1544
D-65800 Bad Soden / Taunus

GIBRALTAR
Mr. Sunder Mahtani
RSSB Charitable Trust Gibraltar
15 Rosia Road

GREECE
Mrs. Eleftheria Tsolaki
P.O. Box 35
Paleo Faliro 17503, Athens

ITALY
Mrs. Wilma Salvatori Torri
Via Bacchiglione 3,   00199 Rome

THE NETHERLANDS
(HOLLAND)
Radha Soami Satsang Beas - Nederland
Middenweg 145 E
1394 AH Nederhorst den Berg

NORWAY
Mr. Sohan Singh Mercy
St. Halvardsgt. 6
N-3015 Drammen

POLAND
Mr. Vinod Sharma
ul. 1go Sierpnia 36 B M-100
PL-02-134 Warszawa, Warsaw

PORTUGAL
Mrs. Sharda Lodhia
Rua Quinta Das Palmeiras, Lote 68
11° andar C, Oeiras 2780-145

ROMANIA
Mrs. Carmen Cismas
C.P. 6-12, Braila-810600

SLOVENIA
Mr. Marko Bedina
Brezje pri Trzicu 68, 4290 Trzic

SPAIN
Mr. J. W. Balani
Calle Panorama no. 15
Cerrado de Calderon
Malaga 29018

SWEDEN
Mr. Lennart Zachen
Norra Sonnarpsvägen 29
S-286 72 Asljunga

SWITZERLAND
Mr. Sebastian Zust-Bischof
Weissenrainstrasse 48
CH 8707 Uetikon am See (ZH)

UNITED KINGDOM
Mr. Narinder Singh Johal
Haynes Park Estate
Haynes, Bedford MK45 3BL

AFRICA

BENIN
Mr. Jaikumar T. Vaswani
01 Boite Postale 951,
Recette Principale, Cotonou

BOTSWANA
Dr. Krishan Lal Bhateja
P. O. Box 402539, Gaborone

GHANA
Mr. Murli Chatani
Radha Soami Satsang Beas
P. O. Box 3976, Accra

IVORY COAST
Mr. Konan N'Dri
08 Boite Postale 569
Abidjan 08

KENYA
Mr. Surinder Singh Ghir
P. O. Box 15134,
Langata 00509, Nairobi

LESOTHO
Mr. Sello Wilson Moseme
P. O. Box 750
Leribe 300

LIBYA (G.S.P.L.A.J.)
Mr. Roshan Lal
P.O. Box 38930, Bani Walid

MAURITIUS
Dr. I. Fagoonee
17 Manick Avenue
La Louise,
Quatre Bornes

NAMIBIA
Mrs. Jennifer Mary Carvill
P. O. Box 1258
Swakopmund 9000

NIGERIA
Mr. Nanik N. Balani
P.O. Box 5054, Lagos

RÉUNION
Ms Marie-Lynn Marcel
5 Chemin 'Gonneau
Bernica, St Paul 97435

SIERRA LEONE
Mr. Kishore S. Mahboobani
82/88 Kissy Dock Yard, P O Box 369,
Freetown

SOUTH AFRICA
Mr. Gordon Clive Wilson
P. O. Box 47182, Greyville 4023

RSSB - SA
P.O. Box 5270
Cresta 2118

SWAZILAND
Mr. Peter Dunseith
P. O. Box 423, Mbabane

TANZANIA
Mr. D.N. Pandit
P.O. Box 1963
Dar-Es-Salaam

UGANDA
Mr. Sylvester Kakooza
Radha Soami Satsang Beas
P. O. Box 31381, Kampala

ZAMBIA
Mr. Chrispin Lwali
P.O. Box 12094
Chingola

ZIMBABWE
Mr. G.D. Wright
Pharmanova, P. O. Box 1726, Harare

MIDDLE EAST

BAHRAIN
Mr. Mangat Rai Rudra
Flat No. 12 Building No. 645
Road No. 2107
Manama 321

ISRAEL
Mr. Michael Yaniv
Moshav Sde Nitzan
D.N. Hanegev 85470

KUWAIT
Mr. Vijay Kumar
P. O. Box 1913, 13020 Safat

U.A.E.
Mr. Mohanlal Badlani
R.S.S.B. P.O. Box 37816,
Dubai

Books on This Science

SOAMI JI MAHARAJ
Sar Bachan Prose
Sar Bachan Poetry (Selections)

BABA JAIMAL SINGH
Spiritual Letters (to Hazur Maharaj Sawan Singh: 1896-1903)

MAHARAJ SAWAN SINGH
The Dawn of Light (letters to Western disciples: 1911-1934)
Discourses on Sant Mat
My Submission (introduction to Philosophy of the Masters)
Philosophy of the Masters (Gurmat Sidhant), in 5 volumes
   (an encyclopedia on the teachings of the Saints)
Spiritual Gems (letters to Western disciples: 1919-1948)
Tales of the Mystic East (as narrated in satsangs)

MAHARAJ JAGAT SINGH
The Science of the Soul (discourses and letters: 1948-1951)

MAHARAJ CHARAN SINGH
Die to Live (answers to questions on meditation)
Divine Light (discourses and letters: 1959-1964)
Light on Saint John
Light on Saint Matthew
Light on Sant Mat (discourses and letters: 1952-1958)
The Master Answers (to audiences in America: 1964)
The Path (first part of Divine Light)
Quest for Light (letters: 1965-1971)
Spiritual Discourses, in 2 volumes
Spiritual Heritage (from tape-recorded talks)
Thus Saith the Master (to audiences in America: 1970)

BOOKS ABOUT THE MASTERS
Call of the Great Master—Diwan Daryai Lal Kapur
Heaven on Earth—Diwan Daryai Lal Kapur
Treasure Beyond Measure—Shanti Sethi
With a Great Master in India—Julian P. Johnson
With the Three Masters, in 2 volumes—from the diary of
   Rai Sahib Munshi Ram

INTRODUCTION TO SPIRITUALITY
A Spiritual Primer—Hector Esponda Dubin
Honest Living: A Means to an End—M. F. Singh
The Inner Voice—Colonel C. W. Sanders
Liberation of the Soul—J. Stanley White
Life is Fair: The Law of Cause and Effect—Brian Hines

BOOKS ON MYSTICISM
A Treasury of Mystic Terms, Part I: The Principles of Mysticism
    (6 volumes)—John Davidson
The Holy Name: Mysticism in Judaism—Miriam Caravella
Yoga and the Bible—Joseph Leeming

BOOKS ON SANT MAT IN GENERAL
In Search of the Way—Flora E. Wood
Living Meditation: A Journey beyond Body and Mind
    —Hector Esponda Dubin
Message Divine—Shanti Sethi
The Mystic Philosophy of Sant Mat—Peter Fripp
Mysticism, The Spiritual Path, in 2 volumes—Lekh Raj Puri
The Path of the Masters—Julian P. Johnson
Radha Soami Teachings—Lekh Raj Puri
A Soul's Safari—Netta Pfeifer

MYSTICS OF THE EAST SERIES
Bulleh Shah—J. R. Puri and T.R. Shangari
Dadu, The Compassionate Mystic—K. N. Upadhyaya
Dariya Sahib, Saint of Bihar—K. N. Upadhyaya
Guru Nanak, His Mystic Teachings—J. R. Puri
Guru Ravidas, Life and Teachings—K. N. Upadhyaya
Kabir, The Great Mystic—Isaac A. Ezekiel
Kabir, The Weaver of God's Name—V. K. Sethi
Mira, The Divine Lover—V. K. Sethi
Saint Namdev—J. R. Puri and V. K. Sethi
Saint Paltu—Isaac A. Ezekiel
Sarmad, Jewish Saint of India—Isaac A. Ezekiel
Sultan Bahu—J. R. Puri and K. S. Khak
Tukaram, The Ceaseless Song of Devotion—C. Rajwade
Tulsi Sahib, Saint of Hathras—J. R. Puri and V. K. Sethi